Prospects for Peacekeeping

Prospects for Peacekeeping

ARTHUR M. COX

THE BROOKINGS INSTITUTION
Washington, D.C.

THE BROOKINGS INSTITUTION
1775 Massachusetts Avenue, N.W., Washington, D.C. 20036

Published October 1967

Library of Congress Catalogue Card Number 67–30590

THE BROOKINGS INSTITUTION is an independent organization devoted to nonpartisan research, education, and publication in economics, government, foreign policy, and the social sciences generally. Its principal purposes are to aid in the development of sound public policies and to promote public understanding of issues of national importance.

The Institution was founded on December 8, 1927, to merge the activities of the Institute for Government Research, founded in 1916, the Institute of Economics, founded in 1922, and the Robert Brookings Graduate School of Economics and Government, founded in 1924.

The general administration of the Institution is the responsibility of a self-perpetuating Board of Trustees. The trustees are likewise charged with maintaining the independence of the staff and fostering the most favorable conditions for creative research and education. The immediate direction of the policies, program, and staff of the Institution is vested in the President, assisted by an advisory council chosen from the staff of the Institution.

In publishing a study, the Institution presents it as a competent treatment of a subject worthy of public consideration. The interpretations and conclusions in such publications are those of the author or authors and do not purport to represent the views of the other staff members, officers, or trustees of the Brookings Institution.

Foreword

Peacekeeping is a term that has come to be associated with the work of the United Nations. It is still controversial, subject to several interpretations, and the focus of a major debate that has not yet been resolved. Peacekeeping is a phenomenon that was not precisely contemplated by the drafters of the United Nations Charter. Most member states have made a distinction between those security operations established to prevent conflict, to observe, and to maintain agreements and cease-fires, and those operations authorized by the Security Council to enforce a decision.

The Soviet Union has insisted that no distinction should be made between peacekeeping operations and enforcement operations because it wishes through the Security Council to maintain maximum control and authority over all operations involving military personnel. It wishes to be in a position to use its veto if it opposes an operation. At the time this book was completed in the spring of 1967, there was no indication that this impasse would be broken. It has existed since the early stages of the UN peacekeeping operation in the Congo and has been exacerbated by the Article 19 controversy and the Vietnam War.

Despite the sharp political controversy, peacekeeping has become the most important aspect of UN action in the field of international security. Thirteen peacekeeping operations have been authorized by the United Nations, including those still in being in Palestine, Kashmir, Cyprus, and between Israel and the United Arab Republic. Measures to strengthen the authorization, management, preparation, and financing of future operations have not moved forward as rapidly as desirable, but progress has been made. In this volume, Arthur M. Cox concludes that peacekeeping operations will continue to be vital to international security, and will be authorized by the United Nations and improvised on a case-by-case basis, even while the controversy over authority and finance continues. He sets forth several steps that can improve US support for international peacekeeping and makes suggestions for strengthening the peacekeeping machinery of the United Nations.

The author relied largely on primary sources including interviews with senior representatives of most of the delegations at the UN; officials responsible for peacekeeping operations in the UN Secretariat; ambassadors representing the Organization of American States, and some of those representing the Organization of African Unity; and senior officials of the White House staff, the Department of State, the Department of Defense, and the United States Delegation to the United Nations.

Prospects for Peacekeeping is part of a program of United Nations Policy Studies financed by a three-year grant from the Ford Foundation to the Brookings Institution. The program is supervised by Arthur M. Cox as part of the Foreign Policy Studies program directed by H. Field Haviland, Jr. Through a series of books, staff studies, seminars, and conferences, this program seeks to propose guidelines for policy and to provide background for more informed public discussion of US participation in international organization affairs.

Arthur M. Cox is a member of the senior staff of the Foreign Policy Studies program of the Brookings Institution. He was previously on the Foreign Policy staff of Brookings in 1947–48. Mr. Cox has had a long career in the United States government, serving in the Economic Cooperation Administration (Marshall Plan) and in the Department of State. Before coming to the

Brookings Institution in 1963, he had been for three years Vice President for International Operations for Frederick A. Praeger, Inc., Publishers. In addition to writing *Prospects for Peacekeeping*, Mr. Cox is co-author, with Karl Mathiasen III, of a 1964 Brookings study entitled *United Nations Institute for Training and Research*. He was a contributor to the Brookings series entitled *Major Problems of U.S. Foreign Policy* in 1947 and 1948.

The author is especially indebted to his research assistant, Larry Fabian, who not only conducted a significant share of the original research and interviews, but wrote most of Chapter 5 as it appears in this volume. Mr. Fabian also made an important contribution with his editorial suggestions. Before coming to the Brookings Institution in 1965, Mr. Fabian worked at the Carnegie Endowment for International Peace. He contributed to that organization's magazine *International Conciliation* and served on its research staff. Mr. Fabian, a member of the Brookings Foreign Policy staff, is currently preparing a study of preparedness for peacekeeping and the earmarking process.

The author and the Brookings Institution are grateful for the helpful comments on *Prospects for Peacekeeping* made by an advisory committee consisting of Arthur W. Barber, Deputy Assistant Secretary of Defense for International Security Affairs; Lincoln P. Bloomfield, Professor, Center for International Studies, Massachusetts Institute of Technology; Andrew W. Cordier, Dean of the School of International Affairs, Columbia University; Elmore Jackson, Vice President, United Nations Association; Joseph Johnson, President of the Carnegie Endowment for International Peace; Porter McKeever, Executive Vice President, United Nations Association; David H. Popper, Deputy Assistant Secretary of State for International Organization Affairs; Francis O. Wilcox, Dean, School of Advanced International Studies, The Johns Hopkins University; and Ambassador Charles W. Yost, Senior Staff, Council on Foreign Relations.

The Brookings Institution and Mr. Cox wish to express particular gratitude to those members of the advisory committee who served on the reading committee: Ambassador Charles W. Yost and Professor Lincoln Bloomfield. Along with Robert E. Asher of the Senior Staff, Foreign Policy Studies program at Brookings, they composed the three-man committee that read the final revised draft of the manuscript and recommended its publication by the Brookings Institution.

The author wishes to express appreciation to Mr. Haviland and Mr. Asher, and to Karl Mathiasen III, also his colleague on the Foreign Policy Senior Staff, who was a stimulating critic and a creative editorial adviser. Mr. Cox also expresses his gratitude to Mrs. Ellen Joseph, who served as editor of the manuscript and made valuable suggestions for its improvement, and to Mrs. Helen B. Eisenhart, who prepared the index. Finally, Mr. Cox gratefully thanks his secretary, Mrs. Pamela Phipps, whose patience, efficiency, and good grace made a major contribution.

The interpretations and the conclusions of the author do not necessarily represent the views of the persons consulted nor of the trustees, the officers, or the staff members of the Brookings Institution or the Ford Foundation.

KERMIT GORDON
President

July 1967
Washington, D.C.

Contents

Prospects for Peacekeeping

AUTHOR'S NOTE: This book was completed before the dramatic events in the Middle East which resulted in the withdrawal of the ten-year-old United Nations Emergency Force on May 18, 1967, and the six-day Arab-Israeli war in June. One of the political problems which faced the United Nations from the outset was that UNEF, though placed as a buffer between Egypt and Israel, was located only on territory of the United Arab Republic. The Israelis did not agree in 1956 to permit the Force on their side of the armistice lines. Thus the continuation of the United Nations presence depended exclusively on UAR consent. When UAR President Nasser requested that Secretary-General U Thant withdraw the Force, two contributors to it, India and Yugoslavia, announced that they would withdraw their contingents unilaterally. U Thant has been criticized by some UN member states for not trying to delay the decision by taking the issue to the General Assembly.

As this is written, there is insufficient evidence upon which to make a sound evaluation of the Secretary-General's action. However, even if there had been some delay due to General Assembly consideration, the results would probably have been no different. In any case, the United Nations again has an important role in the area. Despite UNEF's departure, an expanded UN Truce Observer Mission has been approved by the Security Council. In fact, important progress has been made because the UN truce observers are stationed on both the Israeli and the UAR sides of the Suez Canal cease-fire line.

Undoubtedly the public image of the UN was somewhat tarnished by the turn of events in the Middle East during the summer of 1967. Nevertheless, these events do not change the analysis and recommendations contained in this book. Rather they give an added sense of urgency to the need for making improvements in the authority, the organization, and the command of United Nations peacekeeping machinery. This book considers the alternative means for policing international disputes, particularly from the standpoint of the interests of the United States, and concludes that imperfect though it may be, the United Nations frequently represents the best available alternative.

Arthur M. Cox
July, 1967

1

Peacekeeping and United States Policy

In an article published in *Look* magazine shortly after his death, Ambassador Adlai Stevenson had this to say about peacekeeping:

> I do not underestimate the difficulties of setting up such a policing system. But I believe it is the direction in which we must try to move in the next decade. It could give greater security to the small powers living in the interstices between the great systems. It could restore order in the disorderly regions where power is disputed. It could point the way to the impartial police that one day must take the place of individual arms and the precarious "balance of terror." We must start where we can: and today, of all avenues to security and disarmament, I would place the United Nations' experiments in international peacekeeping at the very head.

Adlai Stevenson, along with Canadian Prime Minister Lester Pearson and UN officials Dag Hammarskjold, U Thant, Ralph Bunche, and others, gave vision, leadership, and meaning to that aspect of international security that has become known as peacekeeping. He knew that no superpower, even one possessing the vast arsenal of the United States, could possibly assume responsibility for policing the world alone. He recognized that the military establishment capable of deterring nuclear aggression is nevertheless unable to prevent small wars, insurgencies, and brushfire disputes. Collective action by many nations had become indispensable to the maintenance of international security.

Since World War II Western Europe has become secure and strong with the help of NATO and the Marshall Plan. Eastern Europe has been under Soviet hegemony and US power has sustained the Monroe Doctrine in Latin America. However, the end of the British Empire and European colonialism left a power vacuum in the Middle East, Southeast Asia, the Indian subcontinent, and Africa that has only partially been filled. These areas have been the locale of much of the warfare of the last decade. An important share of the responsibility for easing these conflicts has been shouldered by the United Nations through peacekeeping operations—in Palestine, between Egypt and Israel, in Lebanon, the Congo, West Irian in Indonesia, Yemen, Cyprus, and Kashmir.

The Meaning of Peacekeeping

What is UN peacekeeping? It is an extraordinary military art because it calls for the use of soldiers not to fight and win, but to prevent fighting, to maintain cease-fires, and to provide order while negotiations are being conducted. A Canadian general who has commanded UN operations refers to peacekeeping as the "process of de-escalation." The soldiers who wear the blue insignia of the UN are politically neutral and not authorized to fire unless fired upon. They are given their mandate by the United Nations—a clear modification of national sovereignty. UN peacekeepers do not intervene in a dispute unless the host government or one of the parties to the dispute calls for assistance or at least consents to the will of the UN majority that a peace force should be sent.

Peacekeeping often is simply the dispatch of a few hundred officers in jeeps to act as observers or fact-finders on a disputed border, as was the case in Greece and Lebanon and still is in Kashmir. Their presence focuses world attention on the dispute and tends to check the expansion of conflict. The larger peacekeeping operations have moved beyond the observer role to the use of organized military units. Until the spring of 1967, the force in the Gaza Strip (United Nations Emergency Force) maintained the cease-fire negotiated after the Suez attacks of 1956 and contributed substantially to the suspension of war between the Arabs and Israel. For ten years troops numbering from 6,000 to the 1967 figure of 3,500 served in UNEF, with contingents from Canada, Brazil, Sweden, Norway, Yugoslavia, Denmark, and India (also Colombia, Finland, and Indonesia in early years).

The peacekeeping operation in the Congo from 1960 to 1964 was the most complex and controversial of them all. During the four-year period its mandate changed from one of maintaining order and ensuring the peaceful departure of Belgian troops to preserving the territorial integrity of the Congo by helping to end the Katanga secession. During the Katanga phase the UN forces returned fire with fire under authority from the Security Council that permitted the use of force to prevent civil war and to apprehend foreign mercenaries. Authority was not granted to employ force to end the secession of Katanga, though one hotly debated and apparently unauthorized action did occur in 1961 that seemed to violate the UN mandate.

Thirty-four states sent a total of 93,000 soldiers to man the mission in the Congo, with major contributions during the operational phase coming from India, Ethiopia, Nigeria, and Tunisia. The entire operation, which cost $402 million, was very small when compared with those in Korea or Vietnam where billions have been expended; nevertheless it precipitated a political and financial crisis. But as Ernest W. Lefever of the Brookings Institution documents in his 1965 volume, *Crisis in the Congo,* contrary to some very critical views of the operation inside and outside the US government, the UN force clearly served the US interest and frustrated Soviet ambitions. It successfully carried out its mission of preventing a deteriorating situation in the heart of Africa from becoming a disastrous international conflict.

The other major peacekeeping operation conducted by the UN has been in Cyprus where about 6,000 soldiers from the United Kingdom, Canada, Finland, Ireland, Denmark, and Sweden have helped to maintain the peace since March, 1964. The military force has been assisted by a few hundred very effective civilian police from Austria, Denmark, Sweden, New Zealand, and Australia. This peacekeeping operation has successfully prevented further fighting between the Greek and Turkish Cypriots and has averted a possible war between Greece and Turkey.

Peacekeepers serve as a deterrent because neither side to a dispute wants to shoot at the UN, nor do the parties to a dispute wish to be charged with aggression. Though the United Nations Charter does provide for enforcement operations under the authority of Chapter VII, which deals with threats to the peace, breaches of the peace, and acts of aggression, the only sanctions authorized by the UN have been the action in Korea (1950–52); the authority granted Britain in April, 1966, to stop, if necessary with force, ships carrying oil for Southern Rhodesia; and, in December, 1966, the decision of the Security Council to impose economic sanctions against Southern Rhodesia, including prevention of oil shipments.

The UN involvement in Korea was a unique occurrence facilitated by the fact that the Soviets had earlier walked out of the Security Council and therefore were not present to veto the action. The United States served as executive agent, providing both military command and political direction, though there was a sixteen-nation UN Advisory Committee. The Korean operation was financed by the US, not by the UN, and the Secretariat had no executive role. In fact, at the outset the United

Nations served as a cover for US action to repel North Korean aggression.]

It is possible that there will be other sanction operations by the UN, but it is unlikely that they will be authorized without the acquiescence of both the United States and the Soviet Union, and even then most infrequently. The more active role for the UN in the security field is likely to continue to be peacekeeping, with authority usually granted by the Security Council, executive responsibility assumed by the Secretary-General, and financing provided through a variety of arrangements.

The Problem of Settling Disputes

Since peacekeeping only checks conflict or maintains a cease-fire, some observers have been critical, claiming that UN operations tend to perpetuate festering sores without healing them, as in Cyprus, Kashmir, and the Arab-Israeli dispute. It is said that the UN peacekeeping operations foster a false sense of security without stimulating the will for settlement. Other critics are unwilling to see money and manpower committed year after year for operations that merely postpone allegedly inevitable aggressive action.

The impatience for settlement has led some people to advocate that disputes be allowed to run their course until one side is in the ascendency. During the 1965 India-Pakistan clash as eminent an observer as former Secretary of State Dean Acheson said that he thought it was better to let them fight it out until a solution was reached, instead of attempting UN or other third-party intervention. There may occasionally be some merit in permitting a small dispute to be resolved by aggressive action or counteraction, but frequently the result is temporary—so unsatisfactory for the defeated party that in time conflict returns. Furthermore, in the world of today there is too much danger of escalation to major war to take the risk of allowing most brushfire conflicts to run their course.

There have been lasting settlements reached through war, but in the era of the Cold War there has always been the possibility that what started as a small war would soon involve one or more of the major powers. In the India-Pakistan conflict the Chinese Communists were backing the Pakistanis. It was partly because of this that the United States was joined by the Soviets in supporting UN action to stop the fighting and block a common enemy's involvement in the subcontinent.

To prefer peacekeeping to some other form of intervention does not exclude using the techniques of peaceful settlement such as diplomacy, conciliation, mediation, and arbitration, which should be pressed at every opportunity. In fact, the peaceful settlement of disputes is essentially the responsibility of the parties, though the UN may assist in various ways. Under Chapter VI of the Charter the Security Council can only recommend terms of a settlement; it cannot force such terms on the parties. Chapter VII permits coercive measures to prevent aggressive action that threatens the peace but it does not provide authority to impose the substantive terms of a political settlement.

Since World War II there have been remarkable negotiated settlements—some of them entirely peaceable. Some high points of diplomacy in the Cold War have been the Austrian Peace Treaty and the partial nuclear test ban. The Soviet withdrawal of medium-range missiles from Cuba, though accomplished with the threat of force, was also a milestone of Cold War negotiation. Significant to the Cold War, too, was the Trieste settlement. Other major diplomatic accomplishments resulted from measures taken in the process of liquidation of the colonial empires of Europe and Britain, particularly the French and British holdings in the Middle East and Africa. The long, bloody war in Algeria was settled by the statesmanship of French President

De Gaulle. Some of the post-colonial arrangements, though, are still the source of major disputes—witness India and Pakistan. The Indonesians have won their independence from the Dutch, and the Belgian Congo has also become independent, though in neither case was the transition well prepared, and in both cases the UN was called in with a peacekeeping operation.

An assessment of the success of various attempts at negotiation in resolving the major disputes since World War II indicates very slow progress. The major unresolved problems in the world today are the divided nations of Germany (with the additional special issue of Berlin), Korea, and Vietnam; the struggle between the Arabs and Israel; the looming collision between Black Africa and the "white redoubt" in southern Africa; the two Chinas of Peking and Taiwan; the issue of Kashmir between India and Pakistan; and the Cyprus dispute involving Greece and Turkey. All of these issues involve a considerable segment of world power either directly or by indirect commitment.

Though there is evidence that the techniques of peaceful settlement have had many successes during the past two decades, that does not mean that all disputes are subject to solution by these methods. But some of the major trouble spots mentioned may be brought to peaceful settlement, and in the meantime where peacekeeping forces exist there is a better opportunity for time and patience to contribute to the healing process. Peacekeeping may in the future keep the lid on some of the other more explosive trouble spots in the world.

The Article 19 Crisis

The United States has profited enormously from UN peacekeeping. In part this explains why the US has supported every UN peacekeeping operation with an affirmative vote. The US has also supplied about 40 percent of the money to finance these programs and substantial logistical support for the larger military operations in Egypt, the Congo, and Cyprus. The US commitment to UN peacekeeping has been extensive not for altruistic reasons, but because these operations have served the national interest. Nonetheless, since the fall of 1964 there has been a noticeable decline in the US commitment, and in US influence and prestige as well. This change undoubtedly was shaped, in part, by the complex battle over financing UN peacekeeping operations in the Congo and the Middle East.

The Soviets and the French, for somewhat different reasons, did not pay their share of the assessed costs of the Congo operation, and the Soviets also refused to accept the obligation to support UNEF. They maintained that the costs assessed by the General Assembly were illegal. The US led a move to take the dispute to the International Court of Justice, which rendered an advisory opinion that the costs of the two peacekeeping operations *were* expenses for which the General Assembly could assess its members. The Seventeenth General Assembly accepted the Court's advisory opinion by a vote of seventy-six in favor, seventeen against, and eight abstentions. But the Soviets and French rejected the Court's advice and still refused to pay, thereby setting the stage for the implementation of Article 19 of the United Nations Charter, which says: "A Member of the United Nations which is in arrears in the payment of its financial contributions to the Organization shall have no vote in the General Assembly if the amount of its arrears equals or exceeds the amount of the contributions due from it for the preceding two full years."

The United States maintained that if Article 19 were not carried out, the Charter would become a mockery and the ability of the UN to conduct peacekeeping operations in the future would be threatened. It was apparent too that more than the necessary two-thirds of the member nations supported the validity of the legal position. However, it was soon obvious that more than law was at stake—this was a fundamental political confrontation between the two superpowers.

The Soviets spread the word that if their vote in the General Assembly were taken away they would withdraw from the UN. The Soviets were hurt by their decisive political defeat in the Congo and asserted that they were not going to contribute to the financial costs of a UN operation that in their judgment was not only illegal, but administered by the Secretary-General and his staff to the advantage of the United States and the detriment of the Soviet Union.

The crucial events in the Congo that precipitated Soviet rage and anguish were those leading to the murder of Prime Minister Lumumba in 1960. The Soviets considered the Congo, in the process of becoming independent from Belgian colonialism, an ideal prospect for Communist penetration in the heart of Africa. Lumumba, who advocated a militant anticolonial policy and who was strongly supported by the more radical African states, was the leader favored by the Soviets. Soviet support included the furnishing of planes, trucks, spare parts, and technicians as well as some rather clumsy and blatant propaganda activity.

Not long after the UN force reached the Congo, President Kasavubu charged Lumumba with plunging the nation into fratricidal war and dismissed him on September 5, 1960. Prime Minister Lumumba countered immediately with a speech on Radio Leopoldville dismissing Kasavubu as President. At this point Andrew Cordier, an American who was a high-ranking UN Secretariat official temporarily serving as Hammarskjold's special representative in the Congo, acted rapidly to avoid violence. He closed all of the major airports and the Leopoldville radio station, thus preventing Soviet planes from airlifting from Stanleyville troops known to be loyal to Lumumba and also preventing further incitement to arms over the radio. Cordier's action was subsequently supported by Secretary-General Hammarskjold.

A few days later on September 14, Mobutu, the Chief of Staff of the Congolese Army, took over the government. At the same time he expelled the Soviet and Czech diplomatic missions on grounds of interference in the internal affairs of the Congo. Lumumba subsequently tried to join his supporters in Stanleyville, but was captured in late November by Mobutu's troops. In February, 1961, Mobutu and Kasavubu arranged to turn him over to President Tshombe of Katanga where, according to the UN Commission formed to inquire into his death, he was executed by a Belgian mercenary. (The irony of history is demonstrated by the fact that General Mobutu, in a second coup in 1965, took over the government again, this time from Tshombe. Since taking power Mobutu has rehabilitated Lumumba, whose death he sealed, as a national hero.)

After the ouster of Lumumba, the Mobutu coup, and the expulsion of the Soviet diplomats, Premier Khrushchev himself appeared at the UN General Assembly with his shoe-thumping speech demanding that Dag Hammarskjold be replaced by a troika consisting of "three persons who would represent the Western, the Socialist and the neutralist blocs." Khrushchev did not have his way, but a continuing attack on the office of the Secretary-General was launched.

When Lumumba was killed early in 1961, the Soviets proceeded with a well-organized campaign, which continues today, to ensure his place in history as a martyr, symbolizing the struggle against colonialism. The school for Afro-Asian students in Moscow was named Lumumba University. When Kenya gained her independence, the first Soviet gesture was to give Prime Minister Kenyatta money to establish a Lumumba Institute. Numerous propaganda devices of this sort have been employed to keep the memory of Lumumba alive. Undoubtedly he would have remained a hero for many Africans without the influence of Communist propaganda, but the Soviets were capitalizing on the opportunity to link the aspirations and sentiment of a large number of Africans with Communist goals.

At the seventeenth session of the General Assembly in 1962, Soviet Foreign Minister Gromyko said:

> Those who bear the responsibility for the present situation in the Congo are attempting to make the Soviet Union and other States pay for the operations of the colonial powers aimed at subverting the independence of the Congo and dismembering that country. Can it be that they want us to pay for the murder of Patrice Lumumba and hundreds of other patriots . . . ? Let no one entertain the belief that the Soviet Union will give a single kopeck or a single cent to help the colonialists sanctify their criminal deeds.

In the meantime, the United Nations was on the verge of bankruptcy because its debt had risen to $150 million, 80 percent of which was caused by the refusal of the Soviet bloc and France to pay their share of the Congo expenses. In desperation the Sixteenth General Assembly in 1961, by a vote of fifty-eight in favor, thirteen against, with twenty-one abstentions, decided to sell $200 million worth of bonds to member governments—these to yield 2 percent interest and be recoverable in twenty-five years with the amortization and interest to be included annually in the regular UN budget. At this point one of the most important developments in the unfolding drama occurred. Those in the Kennedy Administration responsible for submitting draft legislation to Congress authorizing the purchase of the bonds failed to consult in advance with key Republicans—including some Senators especially involved with UN affairs on the Senate Foreign Relations Committee. As a result there seemed to be a strong possibility that US participation in the bond issue would be blocked.

President Kennedy became personally involved and agreed to a compromise drafted by Senator Aiken of Vermont and Senator Mansfield of Montana that provided authority for the US to lend the UN up to $100 million but not to exceed the aggregate amount of loans made by the other nations. The legislation also expressed the sense of Congress that the UN should take immediate steps to ensure continued financial support for the Congo operation. But Congress expected, as part of the bargain, that the Soviets would not be allowed to default on their debt, and it should be stressed that from the outset the commitment to Article 19 had been an integral part of the bond plan as conceived by the Administration.

Congress acted in the fall of 1962. During 1963 there was intensive skirmishing between the Soviets and the Americans. The Soviets sent three deputy foreign ministers touring the capitals of Africa and Latin America carrying the message that if Article 19 were invoked there would be a walkout and the UN would break up. Many of the smaller nations that had supported the legal and financial authority of the Charter began to waver as the politics of the issue became clearer.

By January, 1964, the United States began to indicate concern about the future role of the General Assembly. In his Dag Hammarskjold Address at Columbia University, Secretary of State Dean Rusk expressed the view that there was a need to revise the procedures for authorizing and financing major UN operations. He pointed out that "theoretically a two-thirds majority of the General Assembly could now be formed by nations with only ten percent of the world's population, or who contribute, altogether, five percent of the assessed budget." The United States was obviously concerned that some day it might find itself in the same position as the Soviets, i.e., told to pay for an operation it believed to be against its national interest. In order to forestall this danger, a two-pronged position was evolved providing that a fair share of past debts would have to be paid in accordance with the advisory opinion of the World Court and the terms of the Charter, but that future peacekeeping operations might be financed through several different techniques, including arrangements recognizing that those permanent members of the Security Council who opposed a particular operation could opt out from financial responsibility.

The United States decided to approach the Soviet Union in early March, 1964, with a compromise plan in an attempt to negotiate a solution to the Article 19 crisis. Ambassador Stevenson proposed to Ambassador Fedorenko that a voluntary "rescue fund" be established to restore the UN to solvency. Contributions to the fund would come from paid-up members as well as members in arrears, and the United States itself would make a contribution. The Communist countries and France would pay sufficient amounts to render Article 19 inapplicable for the foreseeable future. (This would mean about $25–30 million for the Soviet Union and about $2–3 million for France, depending on what arrangements were made with respect to bond amortization.) It would be made clear that in contributing to the fund no country was abandoning its interpretation of the Charter with respect to the legality of the Congo operation or UNEF. Finally, to avoid a similar crisis in the future, arrangements would be made to ensure that the Soviet Union and France were never again assessed for a peacekeeping operation they did not wish to support. For weeks there was no Soviet response to this offer of compromise. Finally the answer came: the Soviet Union was not interested in the proposal and would not pay a single ruble of its arrears. In July, 1964, the Soviet Union distributed a lengthy note to UN members publicly confirming its position.

Many governments felt at this point, despite the validity of the legal position, that if the United States were willing to make an exception in the future, it should excuse the past, particularly since it had so clearly gained in the Congo while the Soviets had lost. Nevertheless the US government, fearing adverse repercussions in Congress if it modified its position, decided to press ahead for a showdown on Article 19 when the matter came up in the beginning of the Nineteenth General Assembly in 1964. Edna Kelly, Member of Congress from New York, indicated to the State Department her intention of sponsoring a resolution dealing with Article 19. This concurrent resolution, voted unanimously on August 20, 1964, stated among other things:

> ... it is the sense of the Congress that the President should direct the Permanent United States Delegate to the United Nations to continue efforts toward securing payment by members of the United Nations of their assessments in arrears. . . . if . . . the arrears of any member of the United Nations equals or exceeds the amount of the contribution due from it for the preceding two full years, the President should direct the Permanent United States Delegate to make every effort to assure invocation of the penalty provisions of article 19 of the Charter of the United Nations.

The Soviets were in arrears two years, and the confrontation seemed inevitable. Some observers believe that if the General Assembly had opened on schedule in October, there would have been a two-thirds majority vote favoring the implementation of Article 19. However, because the US elections were coming up and because many nations wanted more time to try to avoid a showdown, the Assembly did not meet until December. US tactics called for pressing ahead for a showdown while remaining ready to grant the Soviets a way out through the "rescue plan." There were rumors that Foreign Minister Gromyko had authority to accept some form of compromise that would avoid the Article 19 collision.

In November the United States provided airlift for Belgian paratroopers to fly from Ascension Island to Stanleyville in the Congo to rescue white hostages held by the rebel forces fighting the government of the Congo. This operation was requested by Prime Minister Tshombe and was perfectly legal as well as humanitarian. However, because Tshombe was considered the puppet of the Belgians by many African governments, the airlift produced an uproar throughout Africa and inspired vitriolic debate in the Security Council where charges of imperialistic aggression and colonialism were hurled against Belgium and the

United States. From that point on, all chances for a two-thirds majority supporting the application of Article 19 vanished.

When U Thant presented a plan whereby all votes would be postponed in the General Assembly, thus avoiding the issue of Article 19, both the US and the Soviets accepted with apparent relief. Thus the Nineteenth General Assembly did nothing. An Afro-Asian compromise plan for settlement of the UN debt was not adopted, but it demonstrated that the Soviets had won the battle. Finally the Albanians, proxy for Communist China, in an attempt to embarrass both the US and the Soviets, broke the no-vote agreement by forcing a procedural vote, which was taken without invoking Article 19, making a travesty of the issue.

The year 1965 brought the unilateral intervention of the United States in the Dominican Republic, which, though later covered by an OAS peacekeeping force and a UN observation group, was considered by most governments to be a violation of the United Nations Charter. The gloom within the UN became even more oppressive during June when President Johnson failed to announce the anticipated modification of the US position on Article 19 at the San Francisco commemoration of the twentieth anniversary of the UN. Then came the tragic and untimely death of Adlai Stevenson, whose vision, dedication, and human touch had made him beloved by his fellow delegates and the personnel of the UN Secretariat, even in the face of some unpopular US policies.

Justice Arthur Goldberg, appointed to succeed Stevenson as Permanent US Representative to the UN, was determined to get the UN moving again before the twentieth session of the General Assembly was convened in the fall. He consulted thoroughly with members of Congress, especially a group of disenchanted members of the House Foreign Affairs Committee, and finally emerged with a position, actually formulated months before, which he was authorized by the President to deliver to the UN Special Committee on Peacekeeping Operations, which had been established in an attempt to break the financial impasse. On August 16, 1965, Ambassador Goldberg said:

> Without prejudice to the position that Article 19 is applicable, the United States recognizes, as it simply must, that the General Assembly is not prepared to apply Article 19 in the present situation and that the consensus of the membership is that the Assembly should proceed normally. We will not seek to frustrate that consensus. . . . At the same time, we must make it crystal clear that if any nation can insist on making an exception to the principle of collective financial responsibility with respect to certain activities of the organization, the United States reserves the same option to make exceptions if, in our view, strong and compelling reasons exist for doing so. There can be no double standard among the members of the organization.

The United States accepted the reality of politics. Since the consensus in the United Nations was opposed to using the sanctions called for by the law of the Charter, the US would abide by the will of the majority. At the same time, however, it put the UN on notice that it was reserving for itself the right to refuse financial support for any future operations to which it was strongly opposed.

Thus, the ideal of collective financial responsibility, shared by the entire membership of the UN and established by the founders at San Francisco, succumbed to the pragmatism of politics. (The Charter drafters had anticipated that important actions by the UN in the field of security would have big-power consent.) Though a majority of governments support the concept of collective financial responsibility, they realize that it is impossible to enforce against one of the superpowers without risking the breakup of the UN. However, as will be shown in Chapter 5 where this subject will be discussed in greater depth, the Article 19 controversy has served a useful purpose by forcing the UN membership to examine the realistic alternatives, which may result in more flexible, less controversial, more politically viable means for financing future peacekeeping operations.

The Changing Position of the United States Toward Collective Security

Since the birth of the United Nations in 1945 the United States has been its prime supporter, its staunchest defender, and its principal source of funds. The US has provided the home for the UN. It has never used the veto in the Security Council, nor has it withheld its support from major operations as have all the other permanent members of the Security Council—the USSR, Britain, France, and Nationalist China.

Opinion polls have consistently shown through the years that 80 percent or more of the US public favors support for UN efforts to maintain the peace. The reasons for this have never been subjected to close scrutiny but one can guess that most Americans favor peace, like motherhood, and the United Nations is supposed to be contributing to peace. Undoubtedly others may give their support for such reasons as having watched dramatic television coverage of UN Ambassador Lodge exposing Soviet shenanigans by displaying the Communist bugging devices discovered at the US Embassy in Moscow, or Ambassador Stevenson revealing the U-2 pictures proving the presence of Soviet missiles in Cuba. Incidents of this sort usually engender support for the organization that is not specific, but all-inclusive. The severe critics are primarily the radical right or those who are disappointed because the Charter does not provide a basis for world government. They represent such a small minority, however, that very few members of Congress have found it politically profitable to consistently attack the United Nations.

Probably the most important reason for the favorable sentiment is that the United States has received very substantial dividends from its investment in the UN. During the first decade the activities that preoccupied the US in the UN involved the Cold War—the heart of US foreign policy was the containment of Soviet-led international Communism. In this connection the

United Nations gave almost 100 percent support to US positions. This is not particularly surprising when it is recalled that the Soviets were engaged in unmistakably aggressive acts that were judged by an organization whose membership was non-Communist or anti-Communist at a ratio of eight to one.

The UN pressed the Soviet Union to get its troops out of Iran in 1946, to stop supporting Greek Communists from across the borders of Yugoslavia, Bulgaria, and Albania in 1947–48, and to stop interfering in the internal affairs of other governments. It served as the umbrella for collective action against the Soviet-backed aggression in Korea from 1950 to 1952, and condemned the brutal repression by the Red Army of the Hungarian Freedom Fighters in the 1956 revolution. The General Assembly served as a useful forum where the United States could expose to the sometimes unwary membership the various subversive activities characteristic of Soviet Cold War tactics.

The UN produced another somewhat unexpected bonus when peacekeeping was developed in 1956. The United States had been shocked when its NATO allies, Britain and France, joined Israel in a carefully planned act of war against Egypt. When the Soviets threatened to send volunteers to fight on the side of the Egyptians, fear of escalation inspired an urgent search for a solution. The United Nations Emergency Force (UNEF) was installed in the Gaza Strip between Egypt and Israel, where it maintained the precarious peace until the spring of 1967.

But, as the Article 19 crisis demonstrated, there have been major changes in the UN and in the US. The UN has burgeoned from an organization of 51 members to 122. Almost all of the new members have emerged from the Afro-Asian world of colonialism as weak, poor, fiercely nationalistic states. They all need development assistance in the form of aid and trade, but because of their colonial experience they fear big-power manipulation. At the same time they want peace between the big powers, in part because they expect this to mean more resources available for economic development. They are generally strong supporters of the UN because it provides a source of multilateral protection and economic assistance in which they can participate and share in the decision-making process.

The UN through the years has been a remarkable reflection of the evolution of its membership. Naturally enough this has been demonstrated by the character and background of the succeeding Secretaries-General. During the early years Trygve Lie of Norway was an excellent, moderate representative of the NATO-dominated majority that implemented most of the business of the United Nations.

Lie was succeeded by Dag Hammarskjold, an economist and philosopher from neutral Sweden, who, though a product of Western culture, was a dynamic leader of the rapidly growing organization whose membership was becoming less concerned with issues of the Cold War than with problems of economic development and national independence. Though accused by the Soviets of violating the impartial role required of an international servant during the Congo crisis, Hammarskjold, with his sensitive antennae, for the most part was able to reflect accurately the true consensus of his times. Premier Khrushchev put it aptly when presenting his troika proposal: "There is no such thing as a completely neutral man." If Hammarskjold had been completely neutral he would have been unable to act—to administer the operations for which he was so effectively responsible. But he was dedicated to the United Nations Charter and was scrupulous about conducting himself as an international civil servant. Though his journal *Markings* shows a mystical inner man, the public man was action personified. He died tragically in a plane crash that occurred as, characteristically, he was on his way to conduct a delicate negotiation in the Congo.

His successor U Thant is a Buddhist from Burma, an independent, neutralist, poor country. His personality and heritage accurately reflect the UN of today. He represents a world no longer dominated by East-West issues, but rather North-South issues—rich versus poor, industrial power versus one-crop economies and over-population, and "have not" colored people versus "have" white people. An indication of just how representative he has been is the fact that all of the major powers, without dissent, asked him to take a second term when, in September, 1966, he announced his intention to retire from office. Support for his continuation was almost unanimous.

The Third World that U Thant symbolizes consists, with Latin America, of more than eighty developing nations. These nations are not a tightly knit bloc, though on matters of common interest, such as trade and aid, colonialism, and race issues, they have tended to vote together consistently. On political issues there is much more diversity since within each region of the world national positions range the spectrum: in the Middle East, Saudi Arabia and Kuwait are conservative while the UAR and Iraq are socialist; in Asia, Thailand and South Korea are on the right but Burma and Ceylon are on the left; in Africa, Guinea and Mali are radical while Liberia and the Ivory Coast are more moderate; in Latin America there are the small military dictatorships and such democracies as Chile and Mexico.

Even though there is still a wide range of political difference within the UN, recent majority sentiment shows growing disenchantment with the United States. This can be explained by several developments. There has been a noticeable shift in US policy with respect to collective measures. After World War II, the United States generally supported collective responsibility in maintaining world security. Thus, the US obtained UN sanction for action in Korea and in the Suez crisis, and used its machinery during the Cuban missile crisis. There were exceptions, however, such as the unilateral intervention in Lebanon and the Bay of Pigs.

Recently, the United States has tended increasingly to act

without first trying to get the support of a UN consensus—witness the unilateral action in the Dominican affair, the airlifting of Belgians to Stanleyville, and the decision to attack North Vietnam by air. The reason is apparent—the United States was confident of receiving support in the earlier crises, and was likely to have been blocked in the more recent situations. But was this just a matter of politics, or had there been support for the US position because there was a very persuasive case in Korea, Suez, and Cuba, and was support lacking now because there was honest doubt about the merits of the US position in the Dominican Republic, the Stanleyville airlift, and the bombing of Vietnam?

It is apparent that a majority of the Third World nations—the major constituency of the UN—is increasingly critical of the US. Until recently the Soviets had been the devils of the UN with their flagrant aggression in Korea, in Hungary, in Berlin, and in Cuba. Since 1963 though, they have been more successful in the UN while the US has been losing ground. They have been given the opportunity to pose as the champion of peace and the opponent of escalation. For years they have also had the additional advantage of supporting all anticolonial measures, many of which the United States has had to oppose or abstain from.

Another important development has been the growing desire to bring Communist China into the UN. Despite the fact that Chinese behavior and lack of interest in meeting the terms of the Charter have been the main impediments, US intransigence on this issue, like the Article 19 fiasco, has given the impression of excessive inflexibility. The United States has also taken what appears to many to be a very negative position on the proposals made by the poor nations in the UN Conference on Trade and Development (UNCTAD). These trends within the UN point to the questions: Has US foreign policy outlived the strategy it set twenty years ago? Is there a danger that present US policies will lead to growing estrangement and isolation from the rest of the world?

In the process of waging the Cold War the United States has built an arsenal of such overwhelming power that its territorial security can be maintained without allies. In fact, there are strong advocates within the country who believe that the US can go it alone when in its judgment action is required to check the spread of Communism, even when such action is opposed by most of the nations of the world.

Others believe the United States does not have the power to go it alone, but that it can implement an effective foreign policy if it cooperates within the Atlantic Alliance. One of the best informed and most articulate spokesmen for this view is Alastair Buchan, Director of the British Institute of Strategic Studies. Writing for the Atlantic Institute in 1966 in a monograph entitled *Crisis Management,* he had this to say:

> The cry of loneliness which Europeans hear from Washington cannot easily be reconciled with what seems to be the real desire of those who actually wield power there, namely, to have complete freedom of choice in an emergency. And as Vietnam has shown, it is difficult for the United States to retain the confidence and support of her forty-two allies in four continents, let alone influential nonaligned powers, if they have had no voice in the decisions which create the particular crisis situation. . . . The United States is, therefore, faced with the same choice in her dealings with the Third World as she wrestled with for many years in Europe, whether to cull the political advantage of working with and through a group of allies or to retain the military advantage of playing a lone hand.

As one step Buchan suggests a new system of multilateral diplomacy, centered in Washington. Several informal groupings of powers would consult regularly as a basis for contingency planning for the potential crises in the various areas of the world. Buchan says: "In a crisis affecting these areas the powers who had committed themselves to such a system of forward planning would expect to play an active part in its solution in the United Nations or by conventional diplomacy." Though this proposal might give some promise of strengthening the fabric of the Atlantic Community it, like many others involving concerted plans and action by the former colonial powers, should be considered carefully before being adopted by the United States, particularly when considering any concerted planning for possible courses of UN action. As soon as any machinery were organized in Washington with membership limited to the major non-Communist powers, it would breed the suspicion of the Soviets and most of the Third World nations. It would undoubtedly be called a "Colonial Club."

One of the arguments advanced by Buchan for the creation of these informal groupings is that though the former European metropoles may not have much military power to add to that of the US in the management of crises, they do have long experience in Asia, Africa, and the Middle East that should be valuable for understanding the politics of some of the disputes. Though it is undoubtedly true that British, French, and Dutch diplomats have important knowledge to contribute, they are tainted in the Third World because of their colonial past. Furthermore, the Third World states believe that if the United States wants expert advice, it should discuss Asian problems with Asians, Arab problems with Arabs, etc., and not with the former metropoles. It should be recalled also that the nations most acceptable for planning and participating in UN peacekeeping operations are not the former colonial powers, but rather those with a reputation for impartiality, such as Canada, Ireland, and the four Nordic states. If the Soviets are to be encouraged to trust and support more UN peacekeeping, the creation of a Washington Club which engages in UN contingency planning would seem to be counterproductive. Regular diplomatic channels in New York, London, and Washington would probably be more prudent lines of communication for US and British talks than any new machinery involving the Western powers.

According to the Department of Defense there have been 164

significant outbreaks of violence involving eighty-two different governments during the last eight years. Most of them occurred in the Third World. Many of them were internal crises involving coups d'état, assassination attempts, riots, and other forms of violence directed at the governments in power. A majority were resolved one way or another so rapidly that they did not become threats to the peace, or subject to international action. A significant number were influenced in their outcome directly or indirectly by US power.

The United States has amassed such power that it can influence the outcome of crises in many ways: it can use the techniques of traditional diplomacy; it can use military force or the threat of military force; it can grant arms or other forms of military assistance; it can grant or withhold economic assistance and food; it can employ the clandestine assets of the CIA; or it can use the Voice of America and the other resources of the US Information Agency. Often several of these techniques and assets will be used simultaneously.

In a move to improve the contingency planning and the coordination of US foreign policy operations, the President early in 1966 created the Senior Interdepartmental Group under the chairmanship of the Under Secretary of State with a membership of the Deputy Secretary of Defense and the heads of CIA, USIA, and AID. Under this top body are Interdepartmental Regional Groups chaired by the Assistant Secretary of State for each region of the world. This machinery strengthens the operational authority of the State Department and focuses in one place the many assets available to the United States in the management of crises.

Crisis management has been concerned primarily with the control and prevention of insurgency and wars of national liberation supported by the Soviets, the Chinese Communists, the Castro forces, or other elements of Communist power such as the Vietcong. The US has decided that the most effective way to avoid such insurgencies is to assist threatened governments to build their own security. Thus, the United States supplies aid to develop or stabilize the economies, and military assistance in the form of weapons and training. It has programs in thirty-three countries to train civilian police in the latest techniques of riot control and prevention of illegal traffic of weapons or personnel. US clandestine programs assist in the training in intelligence and surveillance techniques that can alert governments to threats of coups or insurgencies.

It is notable that, so far at least, the crisis management machinery and contingency planning in the Pentagon have concentrated exclusively on the capability of US assets alone. The United States wants to be able to move swiftly, efficiently, and decisively, with maximum control over the operation. Quite understandably no general or admiral in the Pentagon wants to settle for anything less than full US control and the best and latest weapons. He is responsible to the President, the Congress, and the taxpayer for US security and the lives of American soldiers. This is a fact of military responsibility; it is not necessarily a fact of political reality.

Often US power will not be useful because it will not be politically acceptable to neutralist governments. The United States maintains treaties of alliance with forty-two nations, but there are even more nations that do not want such an alliance. Often leaders of other governments will question the impartiality of the US. When the civil war between the Greek and Turkish Cypriots exploded in 1964, the United States would have been looking for trouble to interpose itself between the Greeks and Turks. Archbishop Makarios would not have entrusted his political fate to the US. He would not accept the good offices of NATO, despite the fact that both Greece and Turkey are NATO members. The United Nations was the only organization he considered sufficiently impartial.

Another consideration that will make the United States hesitate to involve its military force is the risk of direct confrontation with the Soviets. When another feasible alternative is available, it may be prudent to choose it. That is why the United States advised the Congolese government in 1960 to call to the UN for help rather than to the US. More often than not when two nations are in dispute the US will wish to avoid getting in the middle. This is an important reason why it welcomes the UN presence between Egypt and Israel, and in Kashmir between India and Pakistan. The United States would lose politically, possibly disastrously, if it had to use its military power to the advantage of one or the other side in these particular disputes.

Internal subversion and insurgencies in individual nations present harder questions, but usually US power will be useful in such crises only when the government in power is willing to call on the United States for assistance. Political leaders may prefer to call on other friends within their region, or on the UN where they would anticipate a more neutral, more impartial rescuer.

After the Dominican crisis and the escalation in Vietnam the US began to examine the possibility of reliable multilateral alternatives to US action. As will be discussed in Chapter 3, all of the regional alternatives were found wanting. The military pacts—NATO, SEATO, CENTO, and ANZUS—were all conceived as organizations to contain military aggression by the Soviets and the Chinese. They were not devised for peacekeeping and counterinsurgency operations. The regional organizations are not yet ready, if they ever will be, for the policing of brushfire disputes, though they have made important contributions in the conciliation of disputes. The Organization of American States provided a cover for the unilateral US intervention in the Dominican Republic, but this peacekeeping precedent is not a reliable model for the future. The United States has only limited influence in the Organization of African Unity and the Arab League, neither of which shows any prospect of organizing reliable peacekeeping machinery in this decade.

The principal alternative to superpower involvement in policing international disputes is the United Nations. The United Nations has behind it more than twelve years of effective peacekeeping experience supported by more than fifty nations that have contributed troops and materiel (ten of which have earmarked troops for future use). It has a small but able staff of international civil servants in the Secretariat who have managed peacekeeping operations, and a corps of diplomats in the permanent delegations and in some of the foreign offices who have become expert in the politics and the administration of international peacekeeping operations.

Though the United Nations is the best presently available international alternative, the United States seldom considers its use when planning for crisis management. The regional Assistant Secretaries of State are responsible for coordinating plans and operations in their areas, but the Assistant Secretary for International Organization Affairs (UN) has not been assigned a similar responsibility for government-wide planning and coordination of US involvement in, and support for, UN peacekeeping operations. Some of the reasons for this state of affairs have already been discussed; others include a wariness about relying on an organization that may not be able to act fast enough, that is subject to Soviet blocking action, and that is not subject to strong US political control. Notwithstanding these and other drawbacks, which will be discussed in succeeding chapters, the United Nations in the future, as in the past, is likely to provide in certain circumstances the least unattractive alternative to US action.

In May, 1966, Secretary of Defense Robert McNamara, addressing the American Society of Newspaper Editors, spoke on world affairs with wisdom and eloquence. Many observers compared his speech with the 1963 American University address of President Kennedy that set the stage for the partial nuclear test ban agreement. Secretary McNamara said:

. . . neither conscience nor sanity itself suggests that the United States is, should, or could be the global gendarme.

. . . .

The United States has no mandate from on high to police the world, and no inclination to do so. There have been classic cases in which our deliberate non-action was the wisest action of all.

Where our help is not sought, it is seldom prudent to volunteer.

. . . .

The plain truth is the day is coming when no single nation, however powerful, can undertake by itself to keep the peace outside its own borders. Regional and international organizations for peacekeeping purposes are as yet rudimentary; but they must grow in experience and be strengthened by deliberate and practical cooperative action.

These words point the way to the purpose of this volume—an examination of the prospects for peacekeeping.

2

Soviet Policy and Practice

The future of UN peacekeeping will depend, to a growing extent, on the policies of the superpowers—the United States and the Soviet Union. During the UN's first decade, the United States clearly dominated its affairs and was able to muster a substantial voting majority. But as the membership has grown there has been a significant shift in political focus, and Soviet influence has become progressively more of a factor. The balance of power in the politics of the UN has become more nearly equal so that now neither of the superpowers can dominate the Security Council or the General Assembly.

The history of the United Nations has been shaped by two related developments: the Cold War and the gradual liquidation of the European colonial empires. During the early years, when there were only fifty-one members, there was such a preponderance of NATO and Latin American states that US positions were certain to be supported. Therefore the Soviets looked at the UN as a dubious organization within which to wage the Cold War. Their UN policies were essentially defensive, calculated to block actions that would run counter to their objectives in the Cold War. The UN was a very minor factor in the arsenal of Soviet political action—an organization to be used as a propaganda forum, but also an organization to be prevented from effective action in the peace and security field.

Alexander Dallin pointed out in his authoritative volume, *The Soviet Union at the United Nations,* published in 1962, that the official 890-page handbook of the Communist Party, though it included sections on the Korean War and the Suez crisis, did not contain one word about the United Nations. Dallin said:

> The typical Soviet policy has been to keep the United Nations alive but weak. While it has sometimes advocated U.N. action in defiance of other nations' claims of domestic jurisdiction or of regional doctrines elsewhere in the world, Moscow's normal aim has been to safeguard its own freedom of action, to keep the United Nations out of the Communist bloc, and generally to minimize the organization's power.

The Soviet Union's categorical rejection of any UN role during the Hungarian uprising of 1956 was the most dramatic illustration of the above.

The Influence of the Third World

While the Soviet position with respect to UN operations has been essentially defensive, its position on decolonization has been offensive. Through the years the Soviets have been consistent advocates of freedom and sovereignty for the peoples of the colonial territories. Often they have attempted to advance the process of decolonization so rapidly that prospective new nations, unready to govern themselves, would be ripe for Communist influence and exploitation. Whatever their motivation, the Soviets have always taken a stand in favor of the creation of the new nations and against the continuation of the colonial status.

As the new nations have emerged, they have become members of the United Nations. This Third World of more than eighty states has become the prime constituency of the UN, and will undoubtedly continue to be the main beneficiary of UN action. A few weeks before he died, Dag Hammarskjold said, "It is not the Soviet Union, or indeed any other big powers who need the UN for their protection; it is all the others. In this sense the Organization is first of all their Organization." U Thant has stressed the same theme in most of his speeches—that it is the small nations rather than the great powers who have the most to gain from the United Nations. For this and other reasons most of the small states have preferred to stay aloof from the Cold War. They want security and economic development; therefore most of them favor détente between the superpowers. Though the Soviet Union has strongly supported the process of decolonization, it has not succeeded in promoting a pro-Soviet majority.

It is true, however, that as the membership of the United Nations has grown, with a shift in political consensus from pro-West to pro-Third World, the Soviet position has shifted, too, from blocking action to cautious tolerance and acquiescence in certain operations. The Soviets have been particularly interested in trying to woo the Afro-Asian majority that now dominates the General Assembly. Though the Soviets would certainly prefer a pro-Communist vote they are frequently willing to go along with the Third World majority—if not to vote affirmatively for a measure, at least to abstain.

The Third World countries, for their part, have such a large stake in the continuity and strengthening of the UN that most of them wish to do everything possible to avoid a confrontation of the superpowers, which might run the risk of gravely damaging or even destroying the organization. This was clearly demonstrated during the frustrating Article 19 controversy. The politics of the UN are such today that action in the security field is almost inconceivable unless both superpowers at least acquiesce. They both have the veto in the Security Council, and both can probably muster one-third of the membership to block action in the General Assembly to which they are strongly opposed. (Article 18 of the Charter provides that decisions of the General Assembly on "important" questions shall be made by a two-thirds majority.)

It is difficult to imagine a situation in which a two-thirds majority of the General Assembly would override the opposition of the United States or the Soviet Union on any issue that the superpowers considered vital to their interests. The possibility that either power might walk out is such a strong deterrent that the Third World nations are most unlikely to support any action that would run the risk of emasculating the organization. Thus a precarious balance has emerged, with the struggle between the superpowers gradually becoming somewhat muted by the more positive aspirations of the Third World states for various types of action, which they advance in such a way as to avoid superpower confrontation.

How much action is possible under such circumstances? Already the UN has demonstrated a considerable capacity to move ahead with a growing and effective series of programs in the fields of economic and social development and technology. It is in the field of peace and security where progress is harder to come by. Alexander Dallin said in *The Soviet Union at the United Nations* that:

> . . . the Soviet outlook on the United Nations remains unique in some essential ways.
>
> The area of uniqueness lies above all in the Soviet view of the historical process and its translation into action. The profound conviction that, in the long run, neutrality and impartiality are impossible or nonexistent, vitiates the fundamental assumption on which international organizations such as the United Nations are built. The Communist image of the United Nations as an arena of struggle is not a reluctant recognition of a tragic fact, but an exhilarating ride on the wave of the future.
>
> The Soviet view, in sum, combines a revolutionary outlook with a conservative pursuit of its security and a pragmatic effort to make the most of the complex and shifting United Nations scene.

Dallin went on to say:

> Moscow has ignored the fact that the United Nations occupies a far more important place in the thinking and expectations of the developing nations, with regard to their own security and progress. . . .

Since these words were written there has been some change, both in the Soviet sensitivity to the UN aspirations of the Third World states, and also, but less perceptibly, in the Soviet view of neutral operations.

Demands for Security Council Control

Before the spring of 1967, the most explicit statement of Soviet policy was contained in a memorandum dated July 10, 1964, submitted by Soviet Ambassador Fedorenko to the Special Committee on Peacekeeping Operations. Fedorenko expressed the view that a "major contribution would be the achievement of an understanding among States of the UN on the strengthening of the Organization's effectiveness in safeguarding international peace and security." The Soviet statement recognized that, in exceptional cases, it might prove necessary for the UN to employ force and to send armed forces to a disputed area. It asserted that any such action should be taken only as a last resort, and that the Security Council is the only body authorized by the Charter "to adopt decisions in all matters relating to the establishment of UN armed forces, the definition of their duties, their composition and strength, the direction of their operations, the structure of their command and the duration of their stay in the area of operations, and also matters of financing. No other UN body, including the General Assembly, has the right under the Charter to decide these matters." The memorandum went on to say that there must be "agreement of the permanent members of the Security Council on all fundamental matters relating to the establishment, utilization and financing of UN armed forces in each particular case." In other words, the Soviet Union wants to be in a position to use the veto on all matters, including financing and direction, concerning operations that require military personnel. It rules out any role for the General Assembly whatsoever, even in the event that the Security Council is unable to act.

The Soviet position advocated that the long-dormant Military Staff Committee, made up of military chiefs of the Big Five, or their representatives, be given the authority to plan and direct operations authorized by the Security Council involving armed forces. The use of an international committee to conduct military operations, unless it reports to a single commander-in-chief, is the path to certain chaos and impotence. Even in an organization such as NATO, made up of allied nations, a supreme commander is indispensable. A command of five nations, each with the veto, would be an administrative impossibility. All UN operations, so far, have been managed by the Secretary-General, having been authorized either by the Security Council or the General Assembly. The Soviet memorandum did make a slight, though ambiguous, bow in the direction of the Secretary-General, saying, "The Secretary-General, as the chief administrative officer of the UN, should contribute by all means at his disposal to the execution of the relevant decisions of the Security Council." Does this mean that the Soviets would be willing to accept the Secretary-General as the executive authority to implement peacekeeping operations? The record shows that they challenge his authority, and try to control it, but that at the same time they have acquiesced in those operations conducted by him.

The memorandum frequently reiterated the concern that UN security operations be controlled in such a way as to ensure that no particular state or group of states be allowed to carry out its "unilateral aims." This was clearly pointed at the United States. To avoid such an eventuality it proposed that: ". . . United Nations armed forces . . . include, together with contingents from Western and neutral countries, contingents from the socialist [Communist] countries. This means, too, that representatives of the socialist countries would participate in the command of United Nations armed forces. . . ."

The Soviets did take the view, however, that none of the permanent members of the Security Council should contribute contingents to UN armed forces. They urged that other states under the terms of Article 43 of the Charter agree to provide contingents for the use of the Security Council. They said: "In keeping with Article 45 of the Charter, those agreements might make it an obligation of States which have entered into such arrangements with the Security Council to hold immediately available, within their armed forces, certain military contingents and supporting facilities which would be at the disposal of the Security Council." In late 1964 both Czechoslovakia and Bulgaria demonstrated their willingness to carry out the Soviet policy. They declared that they were prepared to place contingents of their armed forces at the disposal of the Security Council and to conclude the appropriate agreements.

The memorandum position on the financing of peacekeeping operations has been sustained inflexibly. Not only have the Soviets refused to pay their peacekeeping debts, but they have remained adamant that the General Assembly has no authority to assess member governments for the cost of any peacekeeping operation. Article 17 of the Charter says, "The expenses of the Organization shall be born by the Members as apportioned by the General Assembly." Some of the member governments subscribe to the view that the peacekeeping costs should be covered by that Article. This is particularly true of some of the smaller governments who are not members of the Security Council and who are concerned to maintain maximum prerogatives and authority for the General Assembly. They are more concerned about the maintenance of the residual authorizing power of the Generaly Assembly than about the power of assessment. The Soviets have held, however, that any question relating to the creation and use of armed forces, including the financing of such forces, is within the exclusive purview of the Security Council. They have further contended that the parties to a dispute should usually be made responsible for paying the costs of a UN force. They have not, however, precluded the possibility that it may be necessary under certain circumstances for the UN members to pay for forces if they are required to maintain international peace and security.

In anticipation of the discussion of peacekeeping scheduled for the special session of the General Assembly in the spring of 1967, the Soviets circulated another memorandum, dated March 16, 1967, which restated many of the points contained in the 1964 memorandum while adding some new positions and some new emphasis. The 1967 memorandum gives special attention to the fact that a growing number of Third World states that are not members of the Security Council have indicated a desire to maintain the authority of the General Assembly for peacekeeping if the Security Council is blocked by the veto. The memorandum notes "that some States threatened by the encroachment of the imperialist Powers on their independence and sovereignty fear that the United Nations will not be in a position to safeguard their security effectively unless the General Assembly is given the power to adopt decisions on peacekeeping operations, binding on all Members of the United Nations, . . ." The Soviets further point out that several states indicated that the Western powers would be unable to prevent the adoption of decisions by the General Assembly whereas in the Security Council they could block necessary peacekeeping operations with the veto.

The Soviets are thus confronted with a new situation in which several of the Third World states think their interests are better protected by strongly supporting the authority of the General Assembly. Since they desire to maintain good relations with these states, they have gone to great pains in their memorandum to warn them against "a dangerous misconception." The Soviets say that the fact that the Western powers support the Uniting for Peace resolution, which interprets the authority of the General Assembly to include peacekeeping, should "put the smaller nations on their guard." They say:

> Is not it a fact that voices are being heard in the United States arguing that the United Nations flag should be used to cover up United States aggression in Viet-Nam? To give the General Assembly such functions would be dangerous to many independent States in Asia, Africa and Latin America, and to the world at large.
>
> . . . .
>
> The principle that the permanent members of the Security Council must be unanimous in taking decisions on questions relating to the maintenance of international peace is important not only for the Soviet Union which is capable of defending itself against any external danger, and not so much for the Soviet Union as for the newly independent States which are not yet firmly established. The Soviet Union cannot agree to the Charter being undermined—and it cannot agree that questions relating to the use of force on the behalf of the United Nations should be referred for decision by a mechanical majority of votes in the General Assembly. . . . The right of veto in the hands of the Soviet Union is an important guarantee of the independence and sovereignty of smaller States. The Arab and other independent States know from their own experience how, in the Security Council, the Soviet Union opposes attacks by the imperialist States on newly independent States.
>
> If the rule of unanimity among the permanent members of the Security Council did not exist, the imperialists could without any difficulty use the United Nations for crushing the national liberation movements of peoples. This is exactly what happened in the Organization of American States when the United States of America succeeded in obtaining authorization from a majority of States members of that organization for United States aggression against the Dominican Republic. It is also a fact that the existence of the principle of unanimity in the Security Council prevented United Nations support being given to Portuguese colonizers who had been thrown out of Goa. Similarly, the existence of this principle prevented the Security Council from taking a decision directed against Indonesia.

In other words, the Soviets are saying that only they can protect the interests of the new nations. They are not willing to risk the two-thirds majority vote in the General Assembly even when that vote may occasionally go against Western interests. They are telling the Third World nations that they must stake their own security on the judgment of the Soviet Union. They are not attempting to provide any alternative for those situations where the Western powers might veto an operation in the Security Council. They are merely reaffirming their view that no action should take place unless there is big-power unanimity. They warn that any exception to the principle could lead to the use of armed forces against the interests of one of the permanent members, thus leading to war. They say, "No international intergovernmental organization should be a sponsor of a new war and thus its own grave digger." It is worth noting that in the reference to Goa the Soviets are rationalizing the aggressive action of India, which was in clear violation of the United Nations Charter; they are also admitting that the Dominican uprising was a national liberation movement.

The Soviet memorandum states that:

> There is yet another important aspect of this question. If decisions on the question of using armed forces on behalf of the United Nations are taken by the General Assembly, this implies that the military operations concerned would be conducted, not under the direction of the Security Council and its Military Staff Committee—as prescribed in the Charter—but under the direction of the United Nations Secretariat. It is not difficult to imagine what consequences this might have, and indeed the consequences which it has had, when such attempts have been made. And quite regardless of the person who holds the office of Secretary-General. Even the most authoritative and impartial figure cannot settle problems which should be settled by States themselves and by their Governments, guided by the Charter.

The memorandum goes on to cite the experience in the Congo to demonstrate the danger of giving too much authority to the Secretariat.

In order to assuage the Third World states, the Soviets propose

> . . . that the newly independent States should be invited to participate to the greatest possible extent in the Security Council's work on the preparation and conduct of United Nations peace-keeping operations. Implementation of these proposals would make it possible for

a large number of these States to participate in the work of the Security Council's Military Staff Committee, in the general strategic direction of a United Nations force created for a given purpose, and in the operational command of this force. These States would also play an important role in the regional bodies which the Military Staff Committee might set up for different regions of the world.

The Soviets say too that they would support measures to enhance the readiness of the Security Council to act swiftly and effectively. Finally, they warn against any further consideration of peacekeeping authority for the General Assembly and state that "if the member states of the UN embark on this road, it would create a situation which would compel the Soviet Union to reconsider its attitude to the activities of the UN."

New Attitudes Toward Participation

At the heart of the controversy over the future of the United Nations lies the question of the willingness of the superpowers to support and contribute to a genuinely impartial Secretariat led by a Secretary-General who strives to represent the Charter and the consensus of 122 disparate, sovereign nations. The Secretariat is the only organ of the UN transcending national interests and national boundaries. It is here that trust and respect must be built if the UN is to act successfully as a world organization representing the collective interests of its members in the maintenance of peace and security.

Article 100 of the Charter says:

1. In the performance of their duties the Secretary-General and the staff shall not seek or receive instructions from any government or from any other authority external to the Organization. They shall refrain from any action which might reflect on their position as international officials responsible only to the Organization.

2. Each Member of the United Nations undertakes to respect the exclusively international character of the responsibilities of the Secretary-General and the staff and not to seek to influence them in the discharge of their responsibilities.

Those states most concerned with promoting the impartiality of the UN have observed the admonition in this Article faithfully. The Soviets and their Communist allies have been the most consistent violators—until recently.

It was generally believed at the UN that Communists assigned to the Secretariat usually took their instructions from their governments and from the Soviet bloc caucus. It was impossible for the Soviets to imagine that a citizen of a nation could be working for an international secretariat and not representing directly and primarily the interests of his government. The Soviets were so convinced of this that they saw no reason not to insert their intelligence agents into the Secretariat—and they occasionally did so.

This became an extremely sensitive matter during the UN peacekeeping operation in the Congo when Dag Hammarskjold created a small advisory group within the Secretariat known as the "Congo Club" that included three high-ranking Americans: Ralph Bunche, Andrew Cordier, and Heinz Wieschhoff. As trusted UN employees they had access to all of the confidential telegrams, and participated actively in the management of the Congo operation. The Secretariat officials from the Communist countries were excluded. This fact, plus the incident when Cordier closed the airfields in the Congo, so outraged the Soviets that they claimed Hammarskjold was an agent of US policy. The Soviets felt that the UN was being used as a partisan instrument against their interests and therefore proposed the troika which, in effect, would have established the veto in the Secretariat, making it impossible to operate. After the death of Dag Hammarskjold the "Congo Club" was discontinued. During the last phase of the Congo operation U Thant kept the Soviets more fully informed, allowing them to see some cables and seeking their advice on various matters.

It is a great testimonial to U Thant that the Soviets not only gave up the troika proposal, but also supported him for a second term. Perhaps equally remarkable is the fact that the Communists, despite holding firm to their public opposition to the role of the Secretariat in peacekeeping, have quietly begun to accept and even to participate in some of these activities of the Secretariat. This has been especially noticeable in the peacekeeping operation in Cyprus. At first the Soviets merely abstained in the Security Council, but more recently they have voted for each six-month extension of the mandate for the operation, though they have not contributed any financial support. In Cyprus for the first time Secretariat officials from Czechoslovakia, Hungary, and Bulgaria have participated in the actual conduct of a UN peacekeeping operation run by the Secretariat in the field. These Eastern European Communists have been responsible for intercommunal negotiations on economic and social affairs, including such potentially sensitive matters as refugee affairs. According to non-Communist observers, they have carried out their assignments effectively and without incident.

During the early stages of the Cyprus operation when the UN force was being formed, the Czechoslovakian government offered to contribute a military unit. (Czechoslovakia and Rumania had volunteered military units to the UN force in the Middle East in 1956, but these were rejected.) If the Czech offer for Cyprus had been accepted, it would have been the precedent-shattering first participation in a UN peacekeeping force by soldiers from the Soviet bloc—soldiers wearing the blue UN insignia and taking their direction from a non-Communist commander under the administration of the Secretariat. But U Thant was pressed by the United States and Great Britain to turn down this offer, perhaps in part because the internal logistics of the Cyprus operation, including communications and supply lines, are dependent on the British bases in Cyprus. The presence of Communist soldiers might have created troublesome intelligence problems. Also, Archbishop Makarios, whose permission was required, possibly preferred not to have Communist troops present.

Whatever the merits of that decision, there is much to be said for greater Communist involvement in UN peacekeeping operations. Experience of this sort builds trust and respect for the impartial manner in which the operations should be conducted. Furthermore, it confirms for both sides that Communists can participate effectively in a nonpartisan operation. It is worth noting that the offer to participate represented a significant switch in Soviet policy. In the past, the Soviets believed that the association of Communist troops with those from free nations over any period of time might have an undesirable political impact. The fact that the Czechs were willing to risk such a possibility while also giving up a small piece of sovereignty to an international operation reflects commendable self-confidence and sophistication. In all probability, the Czech troops would have made an exceptional effort to behave themselves and to create a record for discipline and efficiency. The Soviets have been urging the use of Communist contingents, and their acceptability for further operations is likely to be conditioned by the first performance. The Yugoslav Communists, though not members of the Soviet bloc, have been strong supporters of UN peacekeeping and their troops served most effectively, without incident, in the force in the Middle East. Yugoslav units also served in Yemen and the Congo, though they did pull out of the latter operation for political reasons. If NATO members like Denmark and Norway can serve in UN peace forces, so could Communist states like Czechoslovakia and Poland, so long as they met the standards expected of other states.

When the UN India-Pakistan Observer Mission (UNIPOM) was formed in late 1965, U Thant invited Czechoslovakia, Rumania, Hungary, and Poland to provide military personnel to help supervise the cease-fire. The United States remained silent, for the first time raising no objections to participation of Soviet bloc military personnel in a peacekeeping operation. Though there were early expressions of interest, the Eastern Europeans all declined participation. The Soviets had objected vigorously to the creation of UNIPOM because the Secretary-General had not cleared it in advance with the Security Council. Also, the Soviets had taken a position firmly on the side of India while condemning the Chinese-supported Pakistanis as aggressors. But whatever the reasons for not joining this operation, the precedent has been set for the Secretary-General to invite, without US objection, military personnel of Communist European states to participate in a UN observation operation.

There have been other small but potentially important signs that the Communists may be changing their concept of participation. Several Communist members of the staff of the Secretariat have performed superbly as international civil servants in carrying out their assignments. This can be accounted for, in part, as a phenomenon of UN service; i.e., personnel from whatever nation after a few years at the United Nations tend to develop a loyalty to the organization, a UN point of view, though some still subordinate this to an all-embracing loyalty to their governments. It is also true that the militant, secretive, stand-offish posture of most Soviet bloc personnel during the height of the Cold War has noticeably relaxed, probably because Soviet policy has relaxed.

Some Soviet bloc personnel must have been impressed by the dedication to international service and impartiality so clearly demonstrated by some of their friends from other nations. One of the unsung heroes has been Ralph Bunche, who is an Under-Secretary for Special Political Affairs—the highest ranking American in the Secretariat. The Soviets considered Bunche to be one of the principal villains of the Congo affair. He was accused of being an agent of the US government. Nevertheless, after Hammarskjold's death, Bunche carried on as the man most responsible for the management of the Congo operation. He won the respect and trust of U Thant and has shared with the Guatemalan, José Rolz-Bennett, another Under-Secretary for Special Political Affairs, the responsibility for the day-to-day direction of the Cyprus operation.

It can be observed from the speeches and votes of Soviet officials that the Cyprus operation has won the respect and trust of the Soviet government. Ralph Bunche deserves a large measure of credit for this. Americans conditioned by the Cold War to think of the Soviets as the enemy will wonder why an American international civil servant should be given credit for building Soviet trust and participation. This can be understood only if a central thesis of this book is accepted—that UN peacekeeping operations such as the one in Cyprus, which are in the US national interest, will not be possible in most cases unless *both* superpowers consent to their establishment and unless *both* have positive inducements to continue them.

Another indication of potential change in the Soviet position is their suggestion that they might actively support future peacekeeping operations administered by the Secretariat if there were more socialist (Communist) participation. They have urged that Eastern European units be considered as participants in future operations. They have also explored, off the record, the possibility of greater participation in the command and control of field operations, suggesting consideration of a formula whereby, for example, a UN force might have a Scandinavian commander, with two deputy commanders, one from Eastern Europe and one from the Third World. Critics have charged that this proposal smacks of the troika. It would be prudent, however, not to dismiss it without further exploration. It is not the same as the troika because it provides for a single commander; the troika provides for three co-equal chiefs. If a Communist deputy commander attempted to block the chain of command, he would probably be exposed at once, risking all future participation of Communist units in peacekeeping operations and damaging the Communist political position in the Third World. It would be more realistic to anticipate that an East European deputy commander, like an East European battalion, would make every effort to build a reputation for competence and reliability in the international community. If trust in UN peacekeeping is to grow, some of the risks of greater Communist participation will have to be taken.

Professor Inis L. Claude, Jr., of the University of Michigan, writing in *The United States and the United Nations,* a collection of essays published in 1961, observes that the UN may take pro-Western action, take impartial action, take no action at all, or take pro-Soviet action. Since the Soviets could seldom gain a consensus in support of pro-Soviet action, they usually opted for no action at all. Lately they have supported some neutral action (witness Cyprus and India-Pakistan). The United States has usually pressed for pro-Western action, often successfully, particularly in the first decade of the UN. Recently the US too has backed—in fact, actively supported—neutral operations. Professor Claude believes that if the United States were to concentrate on strengthening the impartial role of the UN, then the Soviets too would tend toward supporting genuinely neutral action in the peace and security field.

Professor Claude says:

My conclusion is that we should discard our preoccupation with the problem of enabling the United States to act against Soviet opposition, in favor of a preoccupation with the problem of convincing the Soviet Union that it is both possible and desirable for the organization to serve the interests of both the major blocs, and of the world at large, by functioning as an Agency for mediating between disputants and for confining the scope and moderating the intensity of the Cold War. The usefulness of the United Nations as an instrument for taking action which we support and the Soviets oppose is small—and is rapidly becoming smaller. It is natural that the Soviets seek to incapacitate the organization for that role, and probable that they can achieve substantial success in the undertaking. This is to say that, in a fundamental sense, the philosophy of the veto which was espoused by the framers of the Charter was, and still is, realistic....

The Effect of Vietnam on Peacekeeping Progress

So long as the war in Vietnam continues, there seems little likelihood that the superpowers will take the steps necessary to improve the UN's peacekeeping machinery. Despite this continuing impasse, however, it is possible for the UN to take peacekeeping action, as it did in 1964 and in 1965 in the Cyprus and India-Pakistan operations. Peacekeeping in the foreseeable future will probably have to be improvised on an *ad hoc* basis, though the know-how, procedures, and personnel could be strengthened. For the time being at least, the financing will usually have to be voluntary, with contributions made by those nations willing and able to give. This is a precarious approach to the funding of something so important as international peacekeeping, but at this stage in history it is probably the only practical solution. Furthermore, it can work, as the Cyprus operation has proven.

During the Twenty-first General Assembly in 1966, the Soviets used delaying tactics and behind-the-scenes diplomatic action to block even the very general recommendations put forward by Canada to clarify the constitutional and financial aspects of peacekeeping. The Soviets, according to representatives from some of the Third World countries, indicated that they would not compromise on any formula to institutionalize peacekeeping so long as the United States continued to bomb North Vietnam. Since the Soviet position has not changed since it was first elaborated by Ambassador Fedorenko, before the bombing of Vietnam began, there is reason to believe that it might be unyielding no matter what transpired in Vietnam.

Nevertheless, the Soviets have shown on several occasions that they are anxious to avoid policies that run counter to majority sentiment among the Third World countries, particularly the Afro-Asian countries. They have also shown great interest in blocking the objectives of the Communist Chinese. As has been noted, the Soviet record on specific peacekeeping operations, such as Cyprus, has always been much more affirmative than their doctrinal position on peacekeeping.

Some day Communist China will undoubtedly be a member of the United Nations. It seems unlikely that she will be admitted if she continues to insist on the take-over of Formosa as a condition to participation. It is possible, though, that with a solution in Vietnam and a guarantee of independence for Formosa, China would take her place as a member, including the permanent seat on the Security Council. As this is written, there is no reason to be optimistic about achieving either condition, but it could happen by the end of this decade. Certainly many UN members have shown a growing inclination to encourage Communist Chinese participation. The main impediment today is the barrier created by the Communist Chinese themselves. Before the Communist Chinese enter the UN, it behooves the superpowers to make sufficient concessions to each other to enable peacekeeping machinery to be strengthened significantly—because after the Communist Chinese move to New York such improvements will probably be much more difficult to accomplish.

3

The Alternatives to United Nations Peacekeeping

Most US planners still tend to think in Cold War terms about controlling international conflict; i.e., containing Communist ambitions. How can the dispute be checked or resolved without permitting Communist penetration or involvement? How can the peacekeeping or enforcement operation be assured of maximum non-Communist control? What available assets can be used securely without the direct involvement of US forces? If US forces should participate in order to provide greater control, what arrangements can be made to share the responsibility to greatest political and military advantage? The answers to all of these questions paint a discouraging picture—there are very few reliable alternatives to the direct involvement of the United States.

United States Allies

The only ally with significant foreign bases and troops abroad with whom there is some joint planning and sharing of responsibility is Britain. Since World War II it has enjoyed a special relationship with the United States that has included not only some nuclear sharing but also a degree of political consultation not present in our relations with any other government. However, as British power has declined there has been an observable decline in the extent to which the United States consults Britain on foreign policy decisions. British foreign commitments have been shrinking each year, with every indication that the process will continue.

The British still have a major NATO troop commitment in West Germany and Berlin numbering between 50,000 and 55,000, but this is being decreased. They have 52,000 men in Malaysia and Singapore and have indicated an intention to keep them there for the duration of the Vietnam conflict. The British base in Hong Kong, protected by 9,000 troops, is also likely to be maintained for a time. In the Middle East, Great Britain's withdrawal from Aden is scheduled for 1968, with further withdrawal imminent in the sheikdoms of the Persian Gulf and the Arabian Peninsula. The bases on Cyprus may not be available much longer, particularly if a settlement of the island's dispute is negotiated.

Since 1962 there has been a rapid reduction in British military commitments in Africa. The proposed defense agreement with Nigeria was dropped when strong opposition emerged within that country. The only remaining defense treaty in Africa is with Libya. At one time Britain had 2,500 men in Libya, but as a result of Arab political pressure this force has been reduced to 1,000, with complete withdrawal under the terms of the treaty scheduled for not later than 1973. There are still small units in the former British protectorates in southern Africa. The only other British commitment in Africa is in Zambia where a limited defense role was assumed in December, 1965, following Rhodesia's unilateral declaration of independence. Great Britain maintains an air squadron in Zambia to airlift oil, assist in defending the Zambian-Rhodesian border, and protect the Kariba dam. The British Navy off Africa totals seven warships, including a carrier. There are still overflight and landing rights in several countries that were formerly colonies.

In 1964, when mutinies occurred in the armies of Kenya,

Uganda, and Tanzania (then Tanganyika) almost simultaneously, those governments called for British help. British troops swiftly restored order, but their presence brought immediate political problems, particularly for President Julius Nyerere of Tanzania. It is difficult for the leaders of newly independent nations to call on the former metropoles for military assistance. It is clear these particular governments will not resort to Britain again if a feasible alternative can be found.

Thus the role of Britain as a substitute or a partner for the United States in policing future conflicts is declining. There is still a lively debate among British policy-makers regarding the most effective and practical future overseas military posture, but as British status declines from that of a great power to a middle power there is growing sentiment in the Government favoring participation in UN peacekeeping.

The only other ally of the United States with a semblance of foreign power is France, and that power is now limited to Germany and Africa. Though De Gaulle made a bid for a joint US, British, French directorate in 1958, he was turned down and France has never acquired the special relationship that the US has maintained with Britain. US-French collaboration on security affairs has steadily retrogressed to the point where French capabilities are no longer given serious consideration in US contingency planning.

Nevertheless the United States is pleased that 63,000 French troops are maintained in West Germany and Berlin. Though French and US policies are at odds in most parts of the world, the fact remains that if crises occur in French-speaking Africa the US would like to see French rather than US troops carry out the firefighting, and would always prefer the French to any Communist alternative. There will probably be occasions, however, when the United States would rather support UN than French peacekeeping, particularly if there is an Afro-Asian consensus calling for UN action.

France maintains defense arrangements with eleven of her former colonies: Dahomey, Mauritania, Senegal, Togo, Gabon, the Malagasy Republic, Niger, the Ivory Coast, Chad, Congo (Brazzaville), and the Central African Republic. French troops were flown to Brazzaville in 1963 during the disturbances that resulted in the overthrow of President Fulbert Youlou. The most controversial intervention occurred in 1964 in Gabon when French forces restored President Leon Mba to power after he had been overthrown in a military coup and imprisoned. At the time, French prestige was damaged throughout French-speaking Africa. As a result of the political repercussions, France has followed a policy of eschewing intervention in disputes involving genuine popular discontent. No attempt was made to become involved in the military uprisings that toppled the governments of Upper Volta, the Central African Republic, and Dahomey in late 1965 and early 1966.

Since 1962 there has been a drastic reduction of about 25,000 French troops stationed in Africa, including 10,500 Africans serving in the French Army. France still maintains about 16,000 troops in Africa, including 4,000 in French Somaliland, smaller units in the independent states of Senegal, Mauritania, Chad, and the Central African Republic, a small base in Algeria, and the nuclear testing grounds in the Sahara. In addition there is a 16,500-man force located in France known as "The Intervention Division" that is highly mobile, prepared to move by air and sea to Africa in response to calls for help.

Also in Africa are more than 80,000 Portuguese troops in the Portuguese territories of Angola, Mozambique, and Portuguese Guinea. Though Portugal is a NATO ally, there is little possibility that the United States will associate its power with Portugal's desire to maintain control of these territories. The same can be said for the 20,000 troops that Spain reportedly maintains in her few small remaining African possessions. The US has gone on record as opposed to continuing colonial domination in

Africa. The United States and Belgium did share the major responsibility for training the Congo Army, and the US provided airlift for Belgian paratroopers during the Stanleyville rescue operation in 1964, but it is improbable that the Belgians will be called back again—though the past seven years have demonstrated that anything is possible in the Congo.

In addition to the dwindling capacity of the European allies, there is the possibility of small but significant military assistance from Asian and Pacific allies. Important contributions have been made in Vietnam by South Korea and Australia, and also New Zealand and the Philippines. It is possible that informal consortia arrangements such as those in Vietnam may set a pattern for future shared security operations in which the United States carries the major responsibility, but this is a fragile basis upon which to plan, particularly in the field of peacekeeping.

The Regional Military Organizations

The oldest, largest, and most powerful of the regional organizations is the North Atlantic Treaty Organization (NATO), which was formed in 1949 to protect Western Europe, including Western Germany, from possible Soviet aggression. NATO is composed of thirteen Western European states plus the United States and Canada. It is a military organization, a defensive alliance produced by the Cold War. NATO has machinery providing for political as well as military consultation among its members. It does not have responsibility for policing disputes involving nonmember Western European countries or even its own members, but in 1956 its members did agree to submit disputes among themselves to the organization's good offices procedures before resorting to any other international agency.

The greatest breakdown in cooperation and coordination in the history of NATO occurred in the fall of 1956 when Britain and France in a secret plot with Israel sprang their attack on Suez. The tragic repercussions of that adventure, which might have been disastrous, were at least partially averted by the successful creation of the United Nations Emergency Force. In December, 1963, when the Cyprus dispute went out of control, three NATO powers, Britain, Greece, and Turkey, all had forces stationed on the island. There was fear that the Soviets might capitalize on the presence of a small but well-organized Communist Party in Cyprus and there was even talk of a "Mediterranean Cuba." For all of these reasons US and British policy-makers favored the creation of a NATO force to establish order on the island. But many of the other members were reluctant, and Archbishop Makarios was categorically opposed to NATO involvement, feeling that a more impartial peace force could be established by the United Nations.

Harlan Cleveland, the US Ambassador to NATO and former Assistant Secretary of State for International Organization Affairs, has suggested "new ways of relating the peacekeeping forces on duty within NATO to the flexible call-up system which the United Nations has been developing for peacekeeping duties elsewhere." The difficulty with Ambassador Cleveland's suggestion is that NATO is considered, quite correctly, to be a partisan, anti-Communist military alliance, which makes it incompatible with the impartial role called for in UN peacekeeping. Further, the Third World states would be reluctant to have an organization dominated by the former colonial powers linked closely with UN affairs. The NATO members that have earmarked personnel for the UN, including Canada, Norway, Denmark, Italy, and the Netherlands, have all been scrupulous in keeping their forces trained for UN service separate from their contingents assigned to NATO.

The other three regional military organizations, the South-East Asia Treaty Organization (SEATO), the Central Treaty Organization (CENTO), and the Australia, New Zealand, US

Pact (ANZUS), have much less potential than NATO for peacekeeping. ANZUS will be implemented only if there is a direct external threat to the security of either Australia or New Zealand. CENTO, whose members are Pakistan, Iran, Turkey, and Britain (Iraq dropped out after the change of government in 1957), was created as a defense against possible aggression from the Red Army, and, like the others, is a Cold War military alliance. The United States, though not a member, has backed CENTO from its inception, which was inspired by Secretary of State John Foster Dulles. An illustration of the impossibility of involving CENTO in peacekeeping was the brief war between Pakistan and India in 1965. Pakistan, instead of consulting with and seeking the support of its CENTO partners, received its principal support from Communist China, while using weapons received from the US ostensibly to defend itself against the USSR. The observers dispatched to maintain the cease-fire came from the United Nations. India, not a member of CENTO, would have quite understandably blocked any involvement of that organization.

SEATO has been useful for the exchange of information and for discussion of the growing Chinese threat, but it has not acted. It was found wanting from the standpoint of US interests when its members failed to support SEATO action in Vietnam. France took a position of outright opposition, and Britain has been unwilling to commit any forces. As Alastair Buchan says in his monograph *Crisis Management:* "Such Western supported collective security systems as do exist, SEATO and CENTO, lack such vitality or authority as NATO has managed to retain, yet NATO cannot and will not act collectively outside its own borders. In consequence, the United States has not found it possible to devise any durable system for collective action or the collective evolution of policy in the areas of the world (Latin America, Africa, the Middle East and Asia) where trouble is most likely to occur."

The Organization of American States

The Organization of American States (OAS) is the only regional organization with a record of considerable experience and success in the control and settlement of disputes. This organization stems from the Inter-American Treaty of Reciprocal Assistance (Rio Treaty) of 1947 and the Charter of the Organization of American States of 1948. The OAS experience in the security field has consisted primarily of employing the techniques of pacific settlement, especially factfinding, observation, conciliation, and mediation. Some of the more important cases in which the OAS used these techniques include: the Nicaraguan aggressions against Costa Rica in 1948 and again in 1955; the Haitian-Dominican Republic dispute of 1949; the situation in Guatemala in 1954; the Honduran-Nicaraguan dispute in 1957; various crises in the Caribbean in 1959 including situations in Panama, Nicaragua, and the Dominican Republic; the dispute between Bolivia and Chile in 1962; the Haitian-Dominican dispute of 1963; the Venezuelan-Cuban dispute of 1963–64; and the dispute between the United States and Panama of 1964.

In addition to this long list of disputes there were two involving exceptional action. The first involved a complaint brought by Venezuela charging the Dominican Republic with aggression. An investigating committee, dispatched in late 1959 by the OAS, found that the Dominican government of Rafael Trujillo had plotted to overthrow the Venezuelan government and had inspired an attempt upon the life of President Betancourt. In a series of actions in 1960 and 1961, the OAS called for breaking diplomatic relations with the Dominican Republic and applying economic sanctions, including embargoes on arms, petroleum and petroleum products, trucks, and spare parts. Trujillo was assassinated in 1961, and six months later the OAS lifted the sanctions. This was the only case of economic sanctions being employed against an OAS member.

The second extraordinary case was the Cuban missile crisis of 1962. Immediately after President Kennedy, on October 22, announced to the world the presence of Soviet medium-range missiles in Cuba and the unilateral US decision to quarantine all offensive military equipment being shipped to Cuba, the matter was taken to the OAS. The Latin American governments responded by unanimously calling for immediate dismantling and withdrawal from Cuba of all offensive weapons. They agreed to take measures, including the use of armed force, to prevent any further weapons reaching Cuba. They also expressed the desire that United Nations observers be sent to Cuba at once.

The OAS action thus converted a unilateral move by the United States into a collective measure and provided a multilateral basis for air surveillance of Cuba, though only the US carried out the flights. Twelve Latin American countries, however, did offer to provide military assistance, naval units, and port facilities to support the operation. The crisis ended six days later without any military action because Premier Khrushchev agreed to dismantle and withdraw the missiles, but the OAS had provided significant political force to the US position, demonstrating solidarity in the hemisphere against any external encroachment.

The only instance of peacekeeping by the OAS was the 1965–66 involvement in the Dominican Republic. The Dominican crisis was caused by revolutionary activity threatening the overthrow of the government. Under the guise of protecting American citizens and other foreign nationals, the United States acted promptly and unilaterally by dispatching marines and then a division of paratroopers. The US did intend to protect its citizens, but a more fundamental reason for the intervention, as later confirmed by President Johnson, was that intelligence reports indicated that the revolutionary forces might be taken over by Communists.

The United States did not discuss its action in advance with the OAS, though some talks were held with individual members. Partly because the matter did not reach the OAS until after the marines had landed, there was an atmosphere of considerable mistrust and even hostility when the subject was debated. Latin Americans have a tradition of profound opposition to any form of intervention by one state in the affairs of another. This tradition dates back to their independence from Spain, but more particularly to the era of Theodore Roosevelt and the "big stick," when the cry of "send in the Marines" became anathema to most Latin Americans. Today the sensitivity on the subject of intervention is broadly based, but is more intense in the democracies and less so in those states governed by the military. So, it was not surprising that the democratic governments of Mexico, Chile, Peru, and Uruguay opposed establishing an OAS peace force in the Dominican Republic; Ecuador also was opposed, and Venezuela abstained. After much arm twisting and disputatious debate, the United States persuaded the OAS to approve by fourteen to six, the minimum vote necessary, the creation of a peacekeeping force—the first one in the history of the OAS. The only Latin member governments willing and able to volunteer contingents for the force were Brazil, Honduras, Nicaragua, and Paraguay—all military governments—and Costa Rica, which sent a token twenty men. Though 85 percent of the force, throughout the operation, was composed of US troops, a Brazilian general was appointed commander. The OAS as an organization had very little responsibility for financing the operation, assuming only some of the administrative costs, which were met with funds contributed voluntarily by some of the members. The cost of the military contingents was borne by the supplying governments, and the United States provided virtually all of the logistical support. In all, the US financed more than 90 percent of the cost.

Many lessons can be learned from the OAS peacekeeping operation—the most important of which are political. Though many of the Latin governments were opposed to the intervention and the continuing presence of US troops, this particular operation probably could not have been carried out by the OAS without substantial US participation and backing. But it was clear that the United States had not learned some important lessons from the experience of the UN peacekeepers. Peacekeeping forces must be expert in preventing fighting. They require special training in riot control and the prevention of civil disturbance. Therefore it did not make sense for the United States to send its most combat-ready, "gung-ho" paratroop division on the Dominican peacekeeping mission.

The UN has learned the importance of ensuring that its peacekeeping forces and their commanders maintain a nonpartisan position. The OAS force was criticized, ridiculed, and occasionally shot at by the revolutionaries. The OAS force was decidedly anti-Communist and the revolutionaries were known to have some Communists among their members. Therefore it was not so remarkable that the OAS commanders tended to share the positions of the Dominican military leaders, Generals Imbert and Wessin y Wessin. This partially accounted for the success in the Dominican cities of the revolutionary campaign that inspired the public outcry, "UN si, OAS no."

On balance the United States preferred the OAS involvement to the alternatives of continued unilateral US policing or a UN peace force. US intervention caused such a furor around the world that the United States became more persuaded than ever that some permanent OAS peacekeeping machinery should be established. There is no provision for any permanent military mechanism in the existing inter-American collective security system, though the Inter-American Defense Board (IADB) was established in 1942 to plan for hemisphere defense against extracontinental aggression. However, the IADB has not even accomplished that limited mission. As one Latin American leader has characterized it: "The IADB is nothing more than a bureaucratic dumping ground. Furthermore, the US members on the Board do not divulge any classified information and therefore continental defense planning is little more than a discussion of theory."

Since 1961 the US Congress has been on record with strong support for an inter-American force. The foreign aid legislation that year incorporated the following advice to the President: "It is the sense of the Congress that an important contribution would be made by the establishment under the Organization of American States of an international military force." Subsequent legislation has made it apparent that if the OAS were to establish such a force, the Congress would appropriate the necessary funds.

There were policy-makers in the executive branch who believed that US influence was sufficiently strong so that even in the face of known opposition a majority would support the creation of an inter-American defense force. The United States did not attempt to add the subject to the agendas, but at the Rio foreign ministers' conference in late 1965, and again at the OAS sessions in Panama in the spring of 1966, it made a strong behind-the-scenes effort to promote the concept. This initiative ran into a stone wall.

Some of the reasons for the Latin opposition can be gleaned from the following remarks made by OAS ambassadors during the course of interviews conducted in the preparation of this book:

> There will be increasing reluctance among a majority of the Latin American governments to use the OAS in any conflict requiring the use of force or even the presence of military personnel. This resistance has been strengthened partly as a result of the "Johnson Doctrine," i.e., that the US will act alone if necessary in order to block the creation of a Communist government in Latin America. This goes back to President Kennedy who said, after the Bay of Pigs, that the US will always act when its national security is threatened and will act alone if its fellow governments in the American states do not agree to par-

ticipate. Kennedy stated that US patience is limited where issues of Communism are concerned. Despite the forthrightness of the "Johnson Doctrine," it can be applied only in the Caribbean. South American governments will no longer tolerate US intervention. Even in the Caribbean it will be most unlikely that the US can obtain the two-thirds vote necessary for OAS action. The Latin American countries will operate essentially on the basis of their historical fear of intervention.

It will never be possible to establish a permanent inter-American force. There are two important reasons. The first is the basic fear of intervention, and the second is that most of the military leaders in Latin America are opposed because they believe that such a force would receive US military assistance presently being given to their own national military establishments.

My government is categorically opposed to any authority whatsoever for the OAS in the coercive field. Any use of force should be authorized by the Security Council of the UN. The OAS will act with military units only in the event of armed aggression from overseas by the Soviets or Chinese. The real issue is how to handle subversive activity within a country which may be given covert external help. There is a great division of opinion within Latin America, with some of the smaller countries genuinely concerned over the prospects of such subversion. The larger Latin countries, on the other hand, have made it clear that they don't want anybody meddling in their affairs even if there is subversive action. The only country which could engage in such meddling is the United States. Any coercive action, whether dealing with subversion, a revolution, or a dispute between countries, must be handled exclusively by the UN.

Some military dictators in Latin America are perpetuating themselves in power under the guise of anti-Communism. A posture of anti-Communism permits them to stay in power in the face of large-scale popular demands for social reform. My government is worried that any sort of inter-American force would be used to quell revolutions which had been inspired by legitimate social demands, merely because those revolutions had some Communists associated with them. The US is so preoccupied with anti-Communism that it mistakenly puts itself in a position of appearing to oppose social progress. If the US concentrates on the question of Communism it will always side with the dictators. The US should give more attention to distinguishing accurately between movements that are actually controlled by Communists and those that are essentially popular. The mistrust of the United States is not based on feelings that the US has imperial ambitions or illusions of territorial conquest, but rather that the US may take irresponsible actions which run counter to genuine aspirations for social progress. My government prefers to have disputes involving the possible use of military forces handled by the Security Council of the UN rather than the OAS. We would always prefer UN intervention to US intervention.

OAS consultation for the Dominican crisis was not inspired by the US but rather by the protest of the Venezuelan government against the landing of US marines. Several of the member governments were so outraged at the US intervention that they were considering calling for direct sanctions against the US. Finally, after calm had been established, a majority of the governments decided to help the US save face. My government believes that the authority of the OAS and the UN run concurrently, with the OAS looked to initially and the UN called upon if OAS action is not possible. Latin Americans should settle their own problems among themselves.

It is still difficult to evaluate the OAS peacekeeping operation in the Dominican Republic as a basis for possible future action. Though most of the critics think the United States should have taken the crisis to the OAS at the outset, there is significant evidence that had this course been followed there would have been no action, because less than two-thirds of the members would have been persuaded of the danger of Communist take-over. Other critics have suggested that after the initial unilateral intervention, the matter should have been handled by the United Nations instead of the OAS. The case was taken to the Security Council by the USSR, which charged the United States with interference in the internal affairs of the Dominican Republic. The US vigorously opposed UN action, preferring the OAS, but finally reluctantly acquiesced in a Security Council resolution calling for a cease-fire and inviting the Secretary-General to send a UN representative to the Dominican Republic to obtain information and make regular reports. The OAS, however, provided the peacekeeping force. If the OAS had not acted and if the United Nations had voted to replace the US troops with a UN peacekeeping mission, it is possible to speculate that a force made up of Canadian, Scandinavian, and Dutch contingents, for example, might have maintained order at least as well as the OAS force. The Soviets might have supported a UN force in preference to continuation of US involvement. However, it is perhaps as likely that the Soviets, seeing the explosive repercussions of the US intervention, would have preferred to leave matters as they were.

In a future crisis the UN alternative might be feasible but in the Dominican crisis of 1965 it was probably out of the question. US public opinion had been aroused to fear another Communist take-over. Even though the Soviets would not have been allowed to influence the make-up of any UN peace force, the fact that they initiated the Security Council action, and the fact that they are so closely linked to Castro's Cuba, would undoubtedly have ruled out US acceptance of a UN alternative.

On balance the OAS peacekeeping operation accomplished its purpose. It did maintain order until a genuine free election could be carried out and then proceeded, after a few months, with the withdrawal of all troops, leaving the new government in full control. The United States was particularly satisfied since the Dominican people chose a government that was free of Communists. In future crises in the western hemisphere involving the use of peacekeeping forces, the US will probably continue to prefer the OAS to the UN. However, an operation such as that in the Dominican Republic probably could not be accomplished by an exclusively Latin American force—the US troops are essential. The fact that US forces are essential to the success of OAS military operations is one of the major reasons why so many Latin American governments are unwilling to institutionalize arrangements for such operations.

In the field of peaceful settlement, however, most of the OAS members prefer OAS rather than UN action. Article 2 of the Rio Treaty says: "... the Parties undertake to submit every controversy which may arise between them to methods of peaceful settlement and to endeavor to settle any such controversy among themselves by means of the procedures in force in the Inter-American System before referring it to the General Assembly or the Security Council of the United Nations." The OAS Charter states that none of its provisions shall be construed as impairing the rights and obligations of the members under the Charter of the United Nations. And the article quoted above from the Rio Treaty is consistent with the United Nations Charter, Article 52 of which says that every effort should be made to achieve settlement of local disputes through regional arrangements before referring them to the Security Council. As already discussed, the problem is not pacific settlement of disputes—the authority and competence of the OAS are well established in this field. The problem arises when military forces are required. Article 53 of the United Nations Charter says: "... no enforcement action shall be taken under regional arrangements or by regional agencies without the authorization of the Security Council." Most Latin American governments strongly adhere to that article, and many of them are inclined to link all use of military forces, including peacekeeping, with that provision. In other words, they believe that the Security Council should authorize all operations involving the use of military forces.

For the foreseeable future it seems unlikely that the OAS can be relied upon as an established mechanism for peacekeeping. The fear of US power, the deep-seated mistrust of any form of intervention, and the concern that anti-Communism may be used to rationalize action that blocks legitimate and desirable social change, all stand in the way of developing a permanent multilateral system for policing disputes in the western hemisphere. Latin American states may be willing to take extraordinary security actions in isolated and exceptional cases, but they are unlikely to agree in advance to an organizational or legal framework for regional action involving the use of military personnel.

The Organization of African Unity

The OAU is the only regional organization, other than the OAS, that may have some prospect as an alternative to UN peacekeeping. Formed in May, 1963, at Addis Ababa, the OAU is very young in experience. Its membership includes all thirty-eight of the independent nonwhite African states. Unlike the OAS, which is dominated by the United States, the OAU has no ties with the major powers. Like the Latin Americans, the African states are preoccupied with the fear of intervention. The OAU Charter sets forth seven guiding principles as follows:

(1) The sovereign equality of all Member-States;
(2) Non-interference in the internal affairs of States;
(3) Respect for the sovereignty and territorial integrity of each Member-State and for its inalienable right to independent existence;
(4) Peaceful settlement of disputes by negotiation, mediation, conciliation, or arbitration;
(5) Unreserved condemnation, in all its forms, of political assassination, as well as of subversive activities on the part of neighbouring States or any other States;
(6) Absolute dedication to the total emancipation of the African territories which are still dependent;
(7) Affirmation of a policy of non-alignment with regard to all blocs.

The strong abhorrence of intervention and the passion for independence reflected in the OAU Charter may explain in part the fact that there have been relatively few border clashes in Africa despite a colonial heritage that left the most irrational boundaries between states found anywhere in the world. President Julius Nyerere of Tanzania said in 1964 in his book, *A United States of Africa:*

> The boundaries which divide African states are so nonsensical that without our sense of unity they would be a cause of friction. We have no alternative, but to start from the position which we inherited from the colonial partition of Africa. There is no one country which does not include areas which would come under another political unit if any principles of political geography were considered, and numerous tribes live in at least two countries or have their origins in some other area of Africa. Yet for us to start making "claims" on each other's territory would be to play into the hands of those who wish to keep Africa weak. . . . In the sphere of boundaries, as in all others, we must start our quest for African unity from the facts of our historical inheritance.

The OAU has not had experience in peacekeeping, in the true meaning of the word, but it has already served well in the mediation of disputes. In 1964 the OAU created a Commission of Mediation, Conciliation and Arbitration. Before that, in late 1963, an *ad hoc* commission was established to deal with the Algerian-Moroccan border war. This commission arranged for the direct mediation by Emperor Haile Selassie of Ethiopia and President Modibo Keita of Mali that produced negotiations leading to a cease-fire. Pressure by organs of the OAU also checked border disputes between Ethiopia and Somalia, Kenya and Somalia, and Ghana and Upper Volta.

The events that provided the impetus for OAU involvement most nearly approximating peacekeeping were the mutinies in the armies of Kenya, Uganda, and Tanzania in January, 1964. As recounted earlier, all of these East African uprisings were put down by British forces that had been called in by the African governments. President Nyerere was embarrassed to have called for help from the former metropole, and felt that since Tanzania was the headquarters for most southern African liberation groups, it was especially inappropriate to have the security and order of his government maintained by British troops. Therefore, just two days after the mutiny was suppressed, he called for an extraordinary session of the OAU Council of Ministers at Dar es Salaam. The Council agreed that even though the uprising had been quelled, the 600 British troops would be replaced within two or three months by an African force of up to three battalions with air support. The troops provided were to be placed under the command and control of the government of Tanzania, which would work out all details with the supplying governments. Thus the new force would not be an OAU force as such, but nevertheless one backed by an OAU resolution. Tanzania approached the governments of Nigeria, Ethiopia, and Algeria. Since Nigeria had a unit just returning from several months of service in the UN Congo force, it was agreed that elements of that unit would go to Tanzania for up to six months. Ethiopia agreed to send a sixty-man contingent of Ethiopian Air Force pilots to begin training Tanzanian pilots. This operation went smoothly and efficiently, resulting in a more stable and effective Tanzanian military establishment.

The OAU has not been successful in advancing toward permanent or earmarked forces that could be used for peacekeeping. Several proposals have been discussed calling for member governments to earmark contingents for a peacekeeping force, but to date they have foundered on such issues as command structure, financial arrangements, location of units, and means for authorizing the use of an OAU force. There has been a wide gap in the positions of the more radical states and the moderates. There are also significant differences in the thinking of many of the newly independent states still protected by military treaties with the French. One of the most important barriers to the development of OAU peacekeeping is that very few of the members have large enough military forces to enable them to send units abroad without risking their own national security. Furthermore, there are even fewer military forces in Africa with sufficient training and experience to operate efficiently in peacekeeping missions.

Of the thirty-eight OAU members, twenty-five have armed forces numbering fewer than 6,000 men. The UAR has a force of 180,000 men but it is primarily involved in security matters relating to Israel and the Arab Middle East rather than Africa. The other North African Arab countries with significant armed forces are Algeria with 48,000, Morocco with 45,000, and Tunisia with 17,000. Elsewhere, Ethiopia has 35,000, Sudan 18,500, Ghana 17,000, Nigeria 11,500, and there are about 35,000 troops in the former Belgian Congo to maintain order in that huge, strife-torn territory. Most of these are relatively small forces to maintain internal security and also be drawn upon for OAU peacekeeping operations. Ethiopia, Nigeria, Tunisia, and Ghana all made significant contributions for lengthy periods during the four-year UN peacekeeping operation in the Congo. Presumably this experience will be valuable for future OAU peacekeeping. As has been observed, it was valuable in the case of the Nigerian contribution in Tanzania. But the toppling of the Nigerian government in 1966 makes it less likely that the small army there can maintain order in that large country, now filled with unrest, and continue to contribute to peacekeeping abroad. For the next few years, at least, the only forces with sufficient size, experience, and stability to contribute to peacekeeping would appear to be the four strongest North African countries plus Ethiopia and possibly Ghana. This is hardly a sufficient base upon which to organize an OAU peacekeeping mechanism even if the politics of the OAU made a force dominated by North Africa feasible, which is not the case.

The single issue of African politics that inspires unity among all OAU members is white domination south of the Zambesi—in Rhodesia, the Portuguese territories, and South and South-West Africa. This so-called "white redoubt," the principal residue of colonialism and racial inequality in Africa, is the source of passionate and virtually unanimous feelings of hatred and outrage among black Africans. The OAU has a "Liberation Committee" that trains exiles from southern Africa in Zambia, the two Congos, and Tanzania. Though some money has been raised and some exile political and military cadres organized and trained, there is little likelihood that the OAU can threaten the stability of the white-controlled governments for many years to come. The lack of military power and organization makes it virtually impotent against the considerable military might of the South Africans, the Portuguese, and the Rhodesians. This will continue to be true unless the OAU states receive outside help from the UN or from one or more of the major powers.

OAU members are well aware of their organization's present limitations, as can be seen from the following statements made during interviews for this book by UN ambassadors representing some of the major OAU states:

> My government strongly favors the OAU as a vehicle for peaceful settlement whenever possible, but when peacekeeping operations involving the use of military units are required we believe that for the time being such operations should be undertaken by the United Nations. It should be possible to link the UN and the OAU in such a way as to avoid the problem of partiality that confronted Hammarskjold when he used African troops in the Congo.

> Our government supports any measures that lead to a stronger UN capability to provide stability in the world. All responsible African statesmen view the roles of the UN and OAU as complementary, rather than as mutually exclusive. We Africans tend to theorize endlessly about African solutions to African problems. However, we are realistic about the drawbacks of the OAU today as an instrument for keeping the peace within Africa. Despite our theorizing we cannot escape the fact that there often will be a clear contradiction between collective peacekeeping under the OAU and the principle of nonintervention that is espoused in the OAU Charter. The bilateral defense arrangements that some African states have with their former metropoles will probably be used very little to maintain the peace. Reliance on France and Great Britain is nothing more than by-passing the UN.

> We are not at all hopeful that any permanent arrangement for earmarking units within the OAU can be reached. There are far too many political divisions among the member states, and it is not clear that any African government would earmark troops for the OAU without knowing precisely what these troops would be asked to do.

We feel that more progress will be made if the OAU concentrates on strengthening peaceful settlement capabilities.

At this stage in history the OAU, like the OAS, seems better suited to conciliation, mediation, and arbitration of disputes. When peacekeeping operations involving military personnel become necessary, neither of these organizations is likely to provide the answer except in the most extraordinary circumstances and then on an *ad hoc* basis.

The Arab League

The Arab League is the only other non-Communist regional organization with experience in collective action to deal with disputes. And that experience is very limited indeed. In 1961 the Arab League did provide a mixed force of three thousand to replace British troops in Kuwait. However, the Arab League has no mechanism to provide earmarked units for Middle East peacekeeping. There is even more political division among the Arab states than exists within the OAS and OAU. What cohesion there is comes from the prevalent sense of injustice caused by the creation of the State of Israel, and from the desire of many Arab nations to eliminate the residue of British influence on the Arabian peninsula and in the Persian Gulf.

These views, which are not shared by the United States, make it clear why the US has never encouraged the Arab League to organize a peacekeeping capability. The Arab world has been the principal locus of UN political and security activity through the years, with UN observation missions in Palestine and Lebanon, UN mediation in most of the Middle East disputes of the past fifteen years, and a UN peacekeeping operation located in the Gaza Strip between Egypt and Israel. The UN will undoubtedly continue to play the leading role in the Middle East because a genuinely operational Arab Union or Arab Peace Force cannot be anticipated during the foreseeable future.

Thus, there are very few promising alternatives to UN peacekeeping for the next decade. The potential of the British and French is rapidly declining. The regional military organizations are not suited for peacekeeping. The only organizations providing some hope for the future are the OAS and the OAU, but that hope is largely in the realm of pacific settlement rather than peacekeeping. Both the OAS and the OAU have demonstrated that in extraordinary circumstances they could provide authority for the formation on an *ad hoc* basis of a peacekeeping force. In both the Dominican Republic and Tanzania, though, the peacekeeping arrangements that were created hardly provide a reliable basis for future crisis planning.

In Asia, Africa, and the Middle East, the United States would prefer to have the UN assume the policeman's role, when it provides a satisfactory substitute for unilateral US involvement. In the western hemisphere, the United States would prefer to see the OAS engage in peacekeeping. However, the Latin fear of US political intervention may often block OAS action. Given a choice between UN action and unilateral US intervention in a dispute in the western hemisphere, the United States has indicated a preference for unilateral action when a threat of Communist take-over looms; in other circumstances the US may acquiesce in a UN presence—particularly if it is supported by a majority of Latin governments.

If the OAS and the OAU do engage in any future peacekeeping operations, even on a completely improvised basis, it would be desirable for them to operate in close collaboration with the UN as provided for in Chapter VIII of the Charter. Article 54 of the Charter says: "The Security Council shall at all times be kept fully informed of activities undertaken or in contemplation under regional arrangements or by regional agencies for the maintenance of international peace and security." The extensive peacekeeping experience of the United Nations might be helpful to the regional organizations.

4

The Peacekeepers

The central purpose of the United Nations as set forth in Article 1 of the Charter is: "To maintain international peace and security, and to that end: to take effective collective measures for the prevention and removal of threats to the peace, and for the suppression of acts of aggression. . . ." Article 43 states: "All Members of the United Nations, in order to contribute to the maintenance of international peace and security, undertake to make available to the Security Council, on its call and in accordance with a special agreement or agreements, armed forces, assistance, and facilities, including rights of passage, necessary for the purpose of maintaining international peace and security." In order to carry out this commitment the Charter provides for a Military Staff Committee, consisting of the Chiefs of Staff, or their representatives, from the five permanent members of the Security Council, that would be responsible for the strategic direction of any armed forces placed at the disposal of the Security Council.

A Permanent United Nations Force

Twenty-two years have elapsed since the drafters of the Charter set forth those goals and there is still no permanent UN force, nor has the Military Staff Committee ever been responsible for the strategic direction of a security operation. The Military Staff Committee, to this day, goes through the motions of convening and adjourning, and the Soviet Union still insists that peacekeeping should be managed through the machinery of the Staff Committee, but that is as far as it goes. The United Nations Charter was drafted in the spirit of euphoria that existed after World War II, though even then Churchill was becoming wary of Stalin's intentions. As the Cold War came clearly into focus it soon became apparent that no UN force could be directed by a committee each of whose members had a veto.

Despite the political reality of the Cold War, the concept of a permanent UN peace force does not die. The Soviets, exploiting the worldwide longing for peace, made propaganda advances during the fifties by calling for a UN force to police a program of universal disarmament. In 1962 the United States responded by proposing a treaty for general and complete disarmament in a peaceful world. Article 4, setting forth the objectives of the proposed treaty, includes among them: "To ensure that during and after implementation of general and complete disarmament, states also would support and provide agreed manpower for a United Nations Peace Force to be equipped with agreed types of armaments necessary to ensure that the United Nations can effectively deter or suppress any threat or use of arms." Objectives such as the foregoing have had the enthusiastic endorsement of the proponents of world government, but critics maintain that such pronouncements are merely the result of propaganda and counter-propaganda, and lead to illusions and possibly cynicism.

In 1957 the Carnegie Endowment for International Peace, inspired by the creation of the United Nations Emergency Force in the Middle East, sponsored a book by William R. Frye called *A United Nations Peace Force*. Frye discussed the possibility of organizing a small permanent UN force of about 7,000 men, with troops contributed by interested member states for periods of six months to two years, during which time they would be stationed at a UN base or in a peacekeeping operation. Thereafter they would be replaced by units from other contributing states. Frye estimated that an adequate base, including training grounds, barracks, air field, depots, and communication and recreation facilities, would cost in the vicinity of $65,000,000, with maintenance and servicing at about $1,000,000 annually. Frye speculated that if the contributing states carried the original costs for equipping the troops with light arms, uniforms, vehicles, and other standard equipment, it might be possible to keep the annual budget for 7,000 men down to $25,000,000.

In 1964, in a volume entitled *International Military Forces,* Lincoln Bloomfield and others examined the feasibility of a permanent force. Bloomfield proposed that "a stand-by force of 25,000 can be made up of single understrength battalions of approximately 500 men each from 50 countries, or of overstrength battalions of 1,000 men from 25 countries. . . . the force could be trained at a facility made available by a neutral country such as India. Approximately 2,500 men would train at any given time, that is to say five 500-man battalions for a period of 6 months. This would result in training 5,000 men a year, or a total of 25,000 in 5 years. . . ." Bloomfield estimates that the annual cost for maintaining such a training command might be as little as $10,000,000.

Though the Frye and Bloomfield proposals are extremely modest both as to size and cost, the UN has not yet moved to establish even a token standby force on a permanent basis. With its present financial crisis, even so small an additional cost as $10,000,000 seems significant. Furthermore, issues such as obtaining an acceptable locus for a base, the selection of a force commander and deputy commanders, and the question of participation by Communist units all are politically sensitive. Even more fundamental is the Soviet and French opposition to additional authority for the Secretary-General. Certainly there is no prospect for an end to this impasse so long as the Vietnam War continues at its present level of conflict. Even before the escalation of the Vietnam War, both Dag Hammarskjold and U Thant, recognizing the major political obstacles, advised against attempting the establishment of a permanent peace force.

In 1948, when it became clear that the Military Staff Committee was making no progress, Secretary-General Trygve Lie proposed a "United Nations Guard Force for guard duty with UN missions, the conduct of plebiscites under the supervision of the UN, and the administration of truce terms. It could be used as a constabulary under the Security Council or the Trusteeship Council in cities like Jerusalem and Trieste during the establishment of international regimes. . . ." Lie estimated that a Guard Force of 800 might cost $4,000,000 a year. This idea finally emerged in watered-down form as a "UN Field Service" of unarmed international civil servants to assist UN field operations in such activities as maintenance of communications equipment and vehicles. (The Field Service has continued to function and in 1966 numbered around 300 including nonpermanent staff detailed to the peacekeeping operations.)

In addition to the UN Field Service, the General Assembly also established a Panel of Field Observers and in 1949 a Panel for Inquiry and Conciliation. Though each member of the UN was invited to appoint one to five persons who might serve on the panels, as a matter of practice the Secretary-General has usually been able to obtain high-level personnel for inquiry and conciliation purposes who were especially suited for a particular assignment, without being limited to names on the panels at the time. In fact, the panels have had very limited use. In 1950 a Peace Observation Commission was established that was composed of the five permanent members of the Security Council and Colombia, Czechoslovakia, India, Iraq, Israel, New Zealand, Pakistan, Sweden, and Uruguay. This Commission was used only once, in 1951–1952 in Greece, when it provided observers to ascertain that outside interference in the affairs of Greece by her Balkan neighbors to the north had ceased. This action was taken when the UN Special Committee on the Balkans (UNSCOB) was being phased out. The United Nations has continued through the years to maintain an active observation role, but has found it more practicable to organize the missions on an *ad hoc* basis than through a permanent commission.

United States Views of the Earmarking Alternative

William R. Frye in *A United Nations Peace Force* analyzes the proposal made by the United States in 1950 during the Korean War, known at the time as the Acheson Plan and since then as the Uniting for Peace resolution. This proposal contained the original call for all member states to earmark troops for UN use. However, shortly after initiating the idea, the United States decided not to earmark troops. Frye says:

One explanation for this decision . . . was that the State Department had lost a long, running battle with the Defense Department, which had not wanted the Uniting for Peace Resolution proposed in the first place. . . . Defense did not believe the UN could or should be relied upon, even in part, for United States security; was fearful that the United States might lose its friendly majority in the Assembly; wanted no action which could lead to de-emphasis of the United States' regional alliances; and did not want its hands tied, even morally, in respect to the future use of any specific element of the United States armed forces. Other opponents, not confined exclusively to the Defense Department, argued that the whole American military establishment would be available to support a UN police action, if we thought the action wise, and that therefore to earmark any specific portion would be to weaken rather than to strengthen the UN. The contrary point of view—that the United States should earmark specific forces—steadily lost ground within the government, though it was vigorously presented. The United States' response would set the pattern for many other states, it was pointed out. At least a token designation of land, naval, and air forces would stimulate other countries to take the same step. If no troops were earmarked by the United States, few would be forthcoming from other countries. These warnings proved only too accurate. The United

States lost its ability to influence other UN members, and Washington found itself in the extraordinary position of having formally urged a course of action in the Assembly, won approval for it, and then been unwilling to take that action itself.

Since 1950 there has been a continuing discussion of the extent to which the United States should participate in peacekeeping. The US has voted for every UN peacekeeping operation and has supplied substantial financial and logistical (particularly airlift) support, but has not earmarked any forces. An important reason for this has been the belief that because of the Cold War it would be the better part of political wisdom not to include military units from the USSR and the US. In 1958 Dag Hammarskjold, setting forth guidelines for UN peacekeeping operations, recommended "that they not include units from any of the permanent members of the Security Council; and not include units from any country which because of its geographical position or for other reasons might be considered as possibly having a special interest in the situation which has called for the operation. I believe that these two principles also should be considered essential to any standby arrangements." Since that time Britain, a permanent member of the Security Council, has participated in the operation in Cyprus under special circumstances. However, neither of the superpowers has participated with military units in any UN peacekeeping operation.

In 1965 a group of Republican Congressmen proposed that the United States earmark a "First Brigade" for UN peacekeeping. They recognized that for political reasons it would not be appropriate to supply infantry troops but suggested that a volunteer unit of approximately 1,000 men be earmarked to provide emergency technical support for peacekeeping operations. They suggested that the unit include: "a company of experts in the establishment and maintenance of communications in crisis conditions, a company of Army and Navy engineers trained in the rapid construction of bridges, roads and buildings; compact and highly mobile medical teams, technical advisors from the Quartermaster Corps to provide rapid information on the supply needs of any peacekeeping operation; an advisory group from MATS (Military Air Transport System, Department of Defense) to provide rapid information on long-range transportation needs, and a sizable staff of multilingual interpreters." They also recommended that the services of MATS should be placed on permanent call to the United Nations for the transport of men and material in any UN peacekeeping operation.

As supporting arguments for their proposal the Congressmen said: "First, it can maximize the efficiency of the technical personnel which the UN may need most urgently and thus give the UN officials confidence that the manpower and skills are available to do a difficult job. Second, and even more important, the 'First Brigade' would be a symbol of this Nation's faith in the UN and its most cherished principles. . . ." This proposal was endorsed by a distinguished advisory committee that included General Lauris Norstad, former Supreme Commander of NATO, and Francis Wilcox, former Assistant Secretary of State for International Organization Affairs. In 1966 the Republican Coordinating Committee recommended that careful study and consideration be given to the proposal to create a "First Brigade." This initiative from the Republicans, however, has not altered the US position on earmarking forces.

President Eisenhower had endorsed the idea of a permanent UN force in his speech to the special session of the General Assembly in the summer of 1958. Again in 1960, in an address to the General Assembly, he said: "I assure countries which now receive assistance from the United States that we favor the use of that assistance to help them maintain earmarked national contingents in the state of readiness suggested by the Secretary-General." The next year, in the Foreign Assistance Act of 1961,

Congress approved the following language, which has remained in the law ever since: "Military assistance to any country shall be furnished solely for internal security, for legitimate self-defense, to permit the recipient country to participate in regional or collective arrangements or measures consistent with the Charter of the United Nations, *or otherwise to permit the recipient country to participate in collective measures requested by the United Nations for the purpose of maintaining or restoring international peace and security. . . .*" [Italics supplied.]

In November, 1965, in his statement before the UN Special Political Committee on the question of peacekeeping operations, Ambassador Arthur J. Goldberg said: "Some countries may be unable to assume the full burdens of training and equipping units for UN service. A program might be organized to train officers and those types of specialized personnel—for example, communications specialists—whose scarcity has hampered previous peacekeeping operations. Aid to earmarking nations could be made available through the UN or through members." Despite the position publicly enunciated since 1960 and the clear authorization of Congress, the United States has not followed through with a program to help other governments earmark, train, and equip units for UN peacekeeping.

The Peacekeeping Nations

There have been efforts to institutionalize UN peacekeeping, and the Charter does provide for the organization of formal machinery. But because of the political barriers UN peacekeeping still operates as an *ad hoc,* improvised response to individual crises. Nevertheless, through the years the United Nations has achieved a remarkable record of effective operation based on the contributions of more than fifty member states, including ten that have specifically earmarked contingents for UN use.

CANADA. The peacekeeping nations are led by Canada, the first member state to earmark a military unit for UN duty. A Canadian brigade known as the Army Special Force was earmarked in 1950, and served in Korea. Since that time more than 30,000 Canadian officers and enlisted men have participated in peacekeeping operations, with the result that men throughout the Canadian military establishment have served under the UN flag. Prime Minister Lester Pearson, a leader in the field, received the Nobel Prize for his contribution to the development of UN peacekeeping. The Canadian White Paper on Defense, written in 1964 and still the guiding policy document, says: "The combined land, sea and air forces normally stationed in Canada and at Canadian ports will be sufficiently flexible to satisfy almost any conceivable requirement for UN . . . operations." This is an exceptional indication of support for UN service that goes beyond that of any other nation.

Canada has by all odds the most developed and sophisticated program for UN military service in existence. Except for the two heavy armored brigades committed to NATO, one in Germany and one in Canada, the entire Canadian armed forces are equipped and trained appropriately for UN operations. In addition, Canada maintains at all times a specially trained 1,000-man battalion earmarked for UN service on a standby basis. Canada selects its personnel for peacekeeping, both officers and men, from the regular standing forces. On matters of finance the Canadian government has been exceptionally generous. Canada absorbs the cost of normal pay and allowances, clothing and personal equipment, including replacement and maintenance, medical inspection, hospitalization on return, and all transportation of the force within Canada. The United Nations is considered responsible for the cost of transportation beyond Canada but so far, in fact, Canada has absorbed all initial costs for air and sea lift required to move Canadian contingents to peacekeeping operations.

Canada has an advanced and highly perfected training program for UN peacekeeping at all levels including courses at the Military Staff College. There is also a special course preparing regimental officers for observer duty. With so many officers having served in UN operations, Canada can usually provide any required number of trained observers even if the number requested exceeds those currently on standby. Canadian officers for observer duty are prepared at all times for service anywhere in the world. They have the necessary medical checkout including shots for yellow fever, cholera, etc. They are trained to write clear and concise reports on military incidents, to operate radio sets, to drive one-quarter and three-quarter ton vehicles, to operate in the field with map and compass, and to survive in conditions as varied as the tropical jungle and the Arctic tundra. In preparation for a specific assignment they also are given a special course in the customs of the theater in which they will serve.

Canadian planning for peacekeeping operates on these assumptions: that units will be required to move quickly in response to crises that develop on short notice; that the role of the UN force will be to maintain the peace by police-type action; that the bulk of the troops will be transported by air, with some heavy and low-priority equipment and stores following by sealift; and that the Canadian contingents will take with them adequate supplies for seven days of operations, with the follow-up supplies arriving by the seventh day. From the first, Canada has taken the lead in providing signals for UN operations. The Canadian battalions operate on the basis of direct and immediate communication between all components, with radio equipment provided even to the rifle platoon and section level. All Canadian contingents have competence in both English and French.

Canadian standby forces are instructed in the rapid loading and unloading of aircraft used by peacekeeping operations. In addition to their regular military training they have special training for peacekeeping actions ranging from police and para-military assistance to military operations for suppressing armed insurgency. The training includes crowd control and dispersal; use of batons and shields; protection of officials, convoys, and buildings; area control including use of road blocks, organizing a cordon and search of buildings, urban patrols, mounting of guards, sweep of areas, and prevention of ambush.

When the Canadian government decides to support a UN operation, the commander of the standby force and some of his officers fly to the overseas theater to review the actual requirements and conditions. Based on his review he decides whether the Canadian contingent is suitable for the task envisaged by the UN commanding officer. If agreement is reached, and it has been in the operations so far, the Canadian force is sent out wearing the blue berets and arm bands of the United Nations.

THE NORDIC FORCE. In the tradition of Dag Hammarskjold, Count Bernadotte, Ambassador Astrom, and numerous other Swedish leaders in UN affairs, Sweden has been second only to Canada in contributing to peacekeeping operations. Through the years more than 20,000 Swedish officers and men have served under the UN flag. Sweden has been closely followed by Norway and Denmark which, though members of NATO, have been consistently strong and impartial supporters of UN operations. These three Scandinavian states in 1961 decided to plan together for earmarked contingents. In 1963 they were joined by Finland in preparing a plan for a "Nordic Standby Force" totalling more than 4,500 officers and men.

Denmark has earmarked one signal company, an infantry battalion of three rifle companies, a staff and technical unit, a military police unit, and a medical company, with a total strength of about 930 officers and men. Norway has earmarked an infantry battalion of 931 officers and men, a frigate from the Norwegian navy with 160 officers and men, and a staff and observer corps of 50 officers. The Norwegian contingents, like those of the rest of the Nordic Force, are planned in such a way as to fill various requirements including linguistic needs. The Norwegian force includes, for example, a maintenance company, a military police platoon, a movement control platoon, and a surgical catastrophy unit.

The Swedish earmarked force consists of two infantry battalions, each totalling 663 officers and men, composed of a headquarters staff and company, three rifle companies, and a supply company. The Swedish plan also calls for an observer contingent, a technical contingent, an air transport division, and a movement control team. The total Swedish contribution is about 1,600 officers and men.

The Swedish plans call for technical capability designed to support certain civilian requirements in the field as well as military and paramilitary operations. The technical contingent will include construction engineers, sanitary squads, pipe-laying squads, electricians, refrigeration and telephone squads, and road and bridge engineers. The air transport contingent will include helicopters, an air transport squadron, mechanics and maintenance personnel, and 30 pilots and navigators. The Swedish contingent is thus able to give help in floods, earthquakes, and other catastrophies. Finland plans to provide one full battalion of 900 to 1,000 men patterned on their battalion presently assigned to the UN operation in Cyprus.

The personnel for the Nordic Force, other than officers, are obtained from volunteers who have completed their required military service and returned to civilian life. They are offered government contracts in which they agree to hold themselves ready for urgent call-up duty in UN operations in which their government has decided to participate. In all of the Nordic countries there are laws prohibiting the use of enlisted personnel in the standing military establishments for overseas duty. These laws are not violated when volunteer forces are employed.

When Sweden earmarked two battalions for UN use, those already assigned to the Middle East and Cyprus forces were the units designated. The battalions in Cyprus and Gaza have been composed of volunteers who signed contracts specifically for service in those operations. They were given special peacekeeping training and then sent on six-month tours of duty. In the future the contracts for UN volunteer service will not be limited to existing peacekeeping operations.

Writing in the July, 1964, issue of *Foreign Affairs,* Per Haekkerup, formerly Foreign Minister of Denmark, outlined several principles that guide the Nordic Force:

> 1. The force shall assist only in peace-keeping operations. This implies that there is no connection between the Scandinavian plan and the provision for enforcement measures contained in Chapter VII of the UN Charter.... The assumption that the Scandinavian standby forces can assist only in the implementation of peace-keeping measures also implies that these forces can never take part in offensive fighting. It is evident, however, that they must have the right to act in self-defense.
>
> 2. A lawfully adopted UN decision is required for the Scandinavian countries to make the earmarked forces available. This must take the form of a request either by the Security Council, by the General Assembly, or by the Secretary-General acting on behalf of either of these bodies.
>
> 3. The country in which the forces are to be used shall have accepted the UN operation and our participation in it....
>
> 4. UN requests can be complied with only after an independent appraisal of the general situation. This implies that the action proposed in the given circumstances must be acceptable to the governments of the Scandinavian countries. This may sound very restrictive and it does, in fact, imply a limitation. It means that the UN will not have the right automatically to draw on the Scandinavian standby force.... But there can be no doubt that our basic attitude to any such request will be a very positive one in keeping with the general lines of our foreign policy in which support of the United Nations forms a decisive element.

5. The force will be placed under the exclusive control of the UN. The only modification here is that it will remain under national jurisdiction in matters of penal law.

OTHER EARMARKING NATIONS. Another country that has made a significant commitment of earmarked forces is the Netherlands. The Secretary-General formally accepted the Netherlands' offer in 1963. It includes a contingent of 600 marines, an armored infantry battalion, a medical company, a supply ship, patrol and scout ships, four regular helicopters and three jet helicopters, a transport plane, and a light armored carrier. The Netherlands, like Canada, has earmarked personnel from its regular military forces. The Netherlands' military contingents, like those of Canada, Norway, and Denmark, are expressly separate from the troop commitments to NATO. The Netherlands' marine contingent is capable of being operated as a unit or broken down into patrols trained for surveillance and reconnaissance. These forces are on standby for twenty-four hour notice and are equipped for self-sustained operations in the field for twenty to thirty days. After this initial period it is anticipated that the UN would be responsible for resupply and logistical support. The Netherlands' marines are trained in amphibious operations and include paratroopers and underwater demolition experts. They are carefully trained in riot and crowd control and various aspects of radio communication. The Netherlands' military staff college provides general instruction for all officers in UN peacekeeping. Though the Netherlands' commitment is substantial, it has not yet been called on to contribute to a peacekeeping operation, perhaps because of a residue of political sensitivity in some parts of the world linked to its colonial past.

The only other states that have specifically earmarked forces for UN service are Austria, Italy, Iran, and New Zealand. Austria is the most recent of the earmarkers, having changed its laws by a parliamentary decision to make the step possible. In late 1966 Austria earmarked a 600-man battalion whose members are two-thirds from the regular army and one-third from the reserves. They are constantly on call, ready to move into a peacekeeping or a disaster operation at the request of the UN Secretary-General or the International Red Cross. The Austrians have already participated in the Cyprus operation, contributing civilian police and a hospital unit.

Iran reportedly intends to commit a battalion too, but the specific plans have not yet been announced. So far, the Italians have specifically earmarked only thirty officers trained primarily for observer use. New Zealand has earmarked less precisely than the others, "a unit drawn either from the armed services or the civilian police." New Zealand has for some time maintained a civilian police unit in the Cyprus operation. Another state that may earmark troops is Switzerland. Recently Switzerland, though not a UN member, has expressed the view that UN peacekeeping as distinguished from enforcement is consistent with her traditional policy of neutrality. If the Swiss government does decide affirmatively, it reportedly may earmark a unit of at least battalion strength for UN use.

GREAT BRITAIN. One of the most dramatic developments in the growing commitment to UN peacekeeping has been the shift of position in British policy. The British government vigorously opposed the UNEF operation in the Middle East and was critical of the Congo involvement, giving only lukewarm support. Since the Cyprus operation, however, there has been a fundamental change. The British have had forces in that operation from the outset, and the British bases in Cyprus have provided the main communications link to UN headquarters. The British participation represents the first time that a permanent member of the Security Council has been included in a peacekeeping operation. British involvement in Cyprus does not provide a solid precedent for the future, however, because the British bases justified an exception to the Hammarskjold guidelines that cautioned against participation in UN peacekeeping by any of the major powers.

Recent trends in British policy indicate that if the British government has a choice, and if the member nations are willing, it would like to follow the lead of Canada toward greater participation in UN peacekeeping. In 1966 Prime Minister Wilson, debating proposed cuts in defense spending east of Suez, claimed that the cuts would come as the government swapped large bases for smaller staging posts, but he argued that if Britain is to help in the peacekeeping role of the UN, then the country has to be on the spot or at least able to get there. In this connection, some British policy-makers are already talking about a UN peace force for Aden when British withdrawal becomes effective in 1968.

Lord Caradon, British Minister of State and Permanent Representative to the United Nations, has been an active and effective proponent of greater British support for UN peacekeeping. Speaking at the United Nations in 1965, he announced that Britain was earmarking logistical support, including airlift, sufficient to equip, supply, and transport six battalions of troops. He said that Britain would also supply personnel for engineering and signals. The British government supplemented these moves with a gift of $10,000,000 to help defray the peacekeeping debt. Thus, Britain has become one of the member states most committed to the advancement of UN peacekeeping.

NONEARMARKING CONTRIBUTORS. In addition to the ten states that have specifically earmarked troops for UN service, more than forty others have participated in peacekeeping operations—in the Congo alone thirty-five nations contributed more than 93,000 men to the UN operation. When it is recognized that many of the member nations have military forces of fewer than

5,000 men, and when it is recalled that the United States, many of the European powers, and all of the Communist bloc countries have not yet participated in peacekeeping, the fact that more than fifty states have contributed troops is an indication that the UN members have shared responsibility on a broadly representative basis.

Among those that have made major contributions are India, Yugoslavia, Brazil, Ireland, Ethiopia, and Nigeria. India has had a unit in the Middle East force (UNEF) since the outset and made available more than a brigade—over 6,000 troops—for the Congo operation. Yugoslavia, though a Communist state, has been proud of its UN service, and has been in UNEF from the beginning and also participated in the Congo and Yemen operations. Brazil has a long and distinguished record, having provided troops in Korea, in UNEF, and most recently in the OAS peacekeeping mission in the Dominican Republic. Ireland has been a participant in the Congo, Yemen, and Cyprus and has actively supported moves to strengthen UN peacekeeping. Ethiopia was second only to India in the size of its force in the Congo and made a very important contribution to the peacekeeping operations that led to the reunification of Katanga with the rest of the Congo. Nigeria too had a splendid record in the Congo, especially its unit of civilian police who were expert in riot control and instrumental in training the Congolese civil police force.

There are many dedicated, hard working, usually unpublicized, and sometimes heroic individual contributors to UN peacekeeping. Among these are international civil servants from the Secretariat who have had major roles in managing the operations both at headquarters and in the field, and some of the Ambassadors to the UN from states that have not yet participated in peacekeeping operations but are nevertheless strong supporters, such as Mexican Ambassador Cuevas Cancino, Chairman of the Special Committee on Peacekeeping Operations, Ambassador Abdul Rahman Pazhwak of Afghanistan, President of the Twenty-first General Assembly, and Ambassador E. R. Richardson of Jamaica.

The fact that so many countries are active supporters and participants in UN peacekeeping and yet have not responded to the Secretary-General's appeal for earmarked units does not reflect any adverse trend or lack of commitment. On the contrary, there has been a steady growth of backing for UN peacekeeping operations despite the Article 19 controversy, the impasse between the superpowers, and the financial difficulties. Some states fear that if they were to earmark they might be placed in an embarrassing position if, for political reasons, they had to turn down a request from the Secretary-General. The earmarking process does not imply any commitment to participate indiscriminately in peacekeeping operations, but nevertheless some of the neutralist nations prefer to avoid the possible political repercussions of being invited to participate in an operation they do not support, or of not being invited when they would like very much to participate. Most of these concerns could be obviated if the Secretary-General always followed the policy of keeping in confidence the names of those states he invites to participate and making public only the list of states that actually agree to make up the force—the general practice of both Hammarskjold and U Thant. Another important consideration for some governments is financial. If the operations continue to depend on voluntary contributions some states prefer not to be placed in the position of pledging units for which there is no certain guarantee of financial reimbursement by the UN. All of these are understandable grounds for not earmarking. Some of them, particularly the financial problem, may in time be overcome, but it seems probable that for the foreseeable future there will always be many more nations willing to support UN peacekeeping who have not earmarked than who have. Nevertheless earmarking remains an important objective, and the

Secretary-General is always in a better position in forming a peacekeeping force when he knows, in advance, that there are a number of nations upon which he can usually rely.

The Lessons of Experience

The United Nations, with twenty years of experience involving more than a dozen operations, has learned a great deal about the art of peacekeeping. But it is still a very fragile art with many imperfections. This must be so in an organization composed of 122 sovereign nations, particularly when it is recognized that each peacekeeping operation must be authorized and formed on an *ad hoc* basis. The possibilities for advance planning and preparation are limited, but certainly more can be done to take advantage of the lessons in past operations.

In the politics of peacekeeping there are several important lessons to bear in mind. The key to successful peacekeeping is genuine impartiality of the peacekeepers. Factors such as color of skin, familiarity with the environment, and geographical proximity are often mentioned as considerations, but are minor when compared with the importance of impartiality. In fact, experience has demonstrated that it is usually better for peacekeepers to be states located at some distance from the host country. Near neighbors often have too much direct interest in the outcome of a dispute. In the UNEF operation located in the Gaza Strip, Egyptian territory adjacent to Israel, there were no Arab states included in the UN force. Clearly Arab participation would have been unacceptable to Israel, and it is also probable that Nasser would have found it politically embarrassing to have Arabs participating in a force located on Egyptian soil.

During the first part of the UN operation in the Congo the force included units from states that were more concerned with the anticolonial aspects of the Congo's transition to independence from Belgium than with impartial service to the United Nations. After Lumumba was overthrown, the United Arab Republic, Indonesia, Mali, Guinea, Yugoslavia, and Morocco abruptly withdrew their contingents totalling more than 6,000 troops and left the Secretary-General and the UN force in a temporarily difficult position. This development was exceptional in the record of UN peacekeeping. In all other operations the participating governments have fulfilled their commitments as long as their service was required. States like Canada, the Nordic powers, and others have developed such a reputation for impartiality that they are acceptable and trusted in most areas of the world.

The management of a peacekeeping operation becomes more difficult when a broad consensus is lacking among the members. If there is large-scale sentiment in favor of an operation, as there generally was for UNEF and Cyprus, then the actual administration both at headquarters and in the field is greatly facilitated. When there is a growing division of opinion, as occurred after the demise of Lumumba in the Congo, the conduct of the operation becomes far more complex. It is remarkable, in fact, that the Congo operation ran as well as it did in the face of strong political pressure from both the more conservative and more radical elements in the dispute. This can be explained in part by the skillful diplomacy of Dag Hammarskjold.

Next to the broad issue of political support and the maintenance of a consensus backing the decisions of the Secretary-General, the most difficult aspect of peacekeeping is the command and control of the force. Since the Congo operation was the largest and most complex in UN experience it has provided the most useful data from the standpoint of guidelines for future operations. In a study prepared for the US Arms Control and Disarmament Agency entitled *United Nations Peacekeep-*

ing in the Congo: 1960–1964, Ernest W. Lefever of the Brookings Institution says:

> . . . the military operation never really got out of control. The command structure developed for the operation, and the supporting communications and intelligence systems may have left a good deal to be desired when compared with that of a competent national army, but the essential fact is that the system worked. . . .
>
> All accounts of . . . the final major operation in Katanga . . . suggest that a highly effective and unified command structure had been achieved.
>
> . . . One factor was the disposition of military officers to obey orders of their military superiors, and the UN Force Commander was their supreme military authority while they were in the service of the United Nations. Further, the governments sending troops to the Congo were anxious to put their best foot forward. They knew the behavior of their units was in the international spotlight. This desire to do a good job in an international operation probably did more to insure the control of the field contingents than explicit orders from the UN Command.

Since the United Nations does not have its own permanent peace force there is no supranational military law or code of discipline to regulate its forces. In matters of discipline each soldier is subject to the discipline of his own contingent commander who in turn follows the regulations of the armed forces of his nation. In the Congo, Lefever says, "Theoretically the UN Command's lack of authority to exercise discipline in serious matters was a great handicap, but in practice, according to the testimony of several Force Commanders, discipline was handled reasonably well." General Indar Jit Rikhye, the Indian who was the Military Adviser to the Secretary-General, wrote in a paper, *Preparation and Training of United Nations Peacekeeping Forces,* that there were: ". . . a few cases, including major crimes, in which the governments concerned were not disposed to make the necessary investigations and to take suitable disciplinary action against the culprits." So long as discipline remains the responsibility of individual governments it is conceivable that the reputation of the UN, or even its operational effectiveness, could be harmed if inadequate discipline were maintained. Based on the record, however, this does not loom as a problem. All of the states that have earmarked troops and most of those others that have been major participants in peacekeeping operations have well-trained, well-disciplined forces. For the future it does mean that the Secretary-General should be cautious about selecting units volunteered by states that have small, relatively inexperienced military establishments.

Communications and intelligence are other sensitive and difficult aspects of operating with international forces. Thanks to the excellent signal units provided by the Canadians, the UN operations have had effective communications. The Canadian load in any future peacekeeping operation may be eased somewhat by the offer of signals support included in the recent British earmarking commitment. Intelligence is a very important and, at the same time, politically sensitive aspect of military operations. The United Nations does not call it intelligence but refers to "military information," which fortunately has not been a significant factor except in the latter stages of the Congo mission. The UN force lacked money to buy information from agents and relied primarily on radio intercepts, air reconnaissance, helicopter and ground patrol, and reports from field liaison officers. An important aspect of effective information and communications in the field is the requirement that at least the officers speak English or French, preferably both, and that some skilled interpreters are available who can communicate in the native language of the country where the peacekeeping operation is located.

There are numerous aspects of logistical support that can be improved if past experience is put to good use. One of the most important is to make advance arrangements for effective and less expensive airlift. This can be accomplished only by analyzing the available sources of transport, the degree of readiness, and the relative costs. Experience has shown that such a study should include both military and commercial airlift alternatives. Another important aspect is stockpiling and standardization of weapons. In the Congo there were several different kinds of rifles all requiring different types of ammunition, which made for a difficult supply problem. The same problem existed with vehicles—at one time there were ninety different makes and types of vehicles all requiring separate spare parts, which made repairs and maintenance a virtual impossibility. Standard procurement at the outset would have avoided this dilemma.

Another important problem to be faced in an operation as large as that in the Congo is the eating habits of the various national contingents. Lefever, referring to the diversity of diets, says: "The Indian, the Ethiopian, the Swede, the Nigerian and all the rest wanted familiar food, and the UN Command, recognizing the obvious morale implications, attempted to meet this need, building on UNEF experience. Under the circumstances, the performance was good."

Still another problem that will be difficult to solve, but may be possible to improve, is the disparity in pay provided for various national contingents. These men are serving under the UN flag together, performing the same duties, but receiving pay based on scales that permit the soldier of one nation to be paid as much as ten times that of another. For example, Swedish troops are paid about $270 a month, plus a monthly overseas allowance of $120, making a total of $390. Indian troops are paid $25 a month plus $8 overseas allowance—a total of $33. Though these pay scales may accurately reflect the differences in the standards of living in Sweden and India, soldiers serving together in the same force are likely to develop a morale problem when there is such a great disparity in pay.

Until there is some sort of permanent UN force there will always be inequities in an improvised force based on national contingents, but the situation might be improved by using certain techniques already tried. For example, in the Congo every soldier serving the UN received an additional $40 a month paid in Congolese currency, which he could use for his personal needs and for purchases at the UN Post Exchange, etc. At the end of his tour he was permitted to convert up to 50 percent of any savings into a hard currency. Furthermore, at the request of the Secretary-General, many governments agreed not to make overseas allowances and salaries available to their men while they were serving in the Congo. The money was held for them and made available when they returned home at the end of their tour.

Research and Training

Clearly, much has been learned about the art of peacekeeping. There have been many strong advocates of a more formal mechanism for utilizing this knowledge to improve future operations. Representatives from several governments believe that field manuals and standard operating procedures could be prepared now that would be invaluable for the peacekeepers of the next decade. They think that the best place to assign this work would be the Office of the Military Adviser of the Secretary-General. But the Soviets, consistent with their opposition to a regular role for the Secretary-General in the management of peacekeeping, have challenged any expansion of the Office of the Military Adviser either as to function or personnel. The Military Adviser, General Rikhye, was detailed to UNEF in 1966 and the staff decreased from three men to one. U Thant has made no attempt to challenge the Soviet position while the Vietnam War continues.

There is some possibility that the United Nations Institute for Training and Research may conduct research in the peacekeeping field that will examine some of the lessons to be learned from past and current experience. For the time being, however, UNITAR is waiting for the completion of an inventory and bibliography of all of the research completed and under way related to the field of peacekeeping. These are being prepared by the World Veterans Federation. After the inventory has been prepared, UNITAR will be in a better position to determine those studies to which it should give priority. In the meantime any operational research or field manuals for peacekeeping will have to be undertaken outside the United Nations.

Since the UN itself has not progressed very far in the operational planning of peacekeeping, those individuals and governments with the most experience have attempted to advance the cause outside the UN framework. In February, 1964, the Norwegian Institute of International Affairs sponsored a private international conference in Oslo to discuss "UN Security Forces as a Means to Promoting Peace." The participants included military officers who had served in peacekeeping operations, administrators who had been responsible for decision-making in international security operations, and scholars. Among the papers presented at the meeting were: "Political and Philosophical Aspects of UN Security Forces," "Central Administration of UN Security Forces," "Establishment of a Staff Element in the UN Secretariat," "Regional Command of UN Security Forces," and "Preparation and Training of UN Peacekeeping Forces." After the conference the "Oslo Papers," as they were called, were published in a book called *Peace-keeping Experience and Evaluation.*

The Oslo meeting was followed in November, 1964, by a conference in Ottawa sponsored by the Canadian government and attended by representatives of twenty-three governments that had earmarked forces or made significant contributions to UN peacekeeping operations. The purpose of the meeting was to explore specific technical and practical operating problems with a view to strengthening the capability of the participating governments to serve the United Nations. There was no discussion of political aspects. Three working groups considered in depth the composition of peacekeeping forces; logistical support of the forces; and personnel administration, public relations, accounting, and legal questions. Discussions at the conference reflected the desirability of establishing standby forces and recognized that such forces would be limited to police duties and would not be used for offensive operations.

In November, 1965, the Norwegian Institute of International Affairs sponsored a second conference in Oslo to discuss earmarked forces for the UN. The main purpose of this meeting was to exchange data among the principal earmarking nations including Canada, the Netherlands, and the four Nordic nations. Subjects discussed at this conference included reports on the status of earmarked forces in each country, and the training, organization, and equipment of earmarked forces. All of these conferences have advanced the cause of peacekeeping by adding to the body of specialized and technical operational knowledge and by bringing together many of the military men and civilian administrators most experienced in the conduct of the various UN peacekeeping operations. They have begun to develop an esprit and mutual respect that are indispensable in the conduct of any international operation.

Though progress has been made, there remains a need for training manuals and standard operating procedures. One important step in this direction has been taken by the Canadian government. The Canadians have prepared a paper dealing with the organization and training of Canadian military forces earmarked for service in UN peacekeeping operations. This paper contains details of the most advanced approach to preparation for such service. It has been informally circulated to interested member governments of the United Nations. The Canadian experience is exceptional and cannot be duplicated by most other governments, but there are many aspects of the Canadian program that can be usefully pursued by other earmarking states, even those with relatively small military forces. For the time being it appears that initiatives such as those taken in Canada and Norway provide the best means for advancing the status of peacekeeping—until the United Nations is prepared to take on the responsibility itself.

Some Practical Measures for the Future

There are other aspects of peacekeeping that also require more attention in preparation for future operations. An important one is the use of civilian police. Already nations such as Nigeria, Australia, New Zealand, and Austria have made important contributions of civilian police to the Congo and Cyprus operations. Since peacekeeping operations are primarily concerned with police-type functions rather than enforcement, some observers have raised the question of whether greater consideration should be given to employment of civilian police in UN operations. Civilian police have special training and skills in such matters as crowd control, control of illegal movement of personnel and weapons, surveillance, and the maintenance of order in urban centers when existing civilian authorities require assistance. The case has been made that in certain peacekeeping operations it would be preferable not to employ military units at all, because the operational requirements are not primarily military in nature.

The Canadians, on the other hand, believe that police duties required in peacekeeping operations can better be handled by military police. They believe that UN peacekeepers should have the military training that will equip them to act calmly and efficiently in the face of the warlike conditions that sometimes prevail. They note that military units have a self-sufficiency that enables them to exist under the most adverse living conditions. They believe further that it is easier to train military units for police duty and assisting civilian authority, than it is to make infantry units out of civilian police. However, proponents of the use of civilian police claim that the military make poor policemen—most military are trained to fight rather than to prevent fighting. They maintain that police are better trained to check small insurgencies in their beginning stages. British-trained civilian police have been effective in controlling insurgency in Asia and the Middle East. As to self-sufficiency, British experts claim that a civilian policeman can better exist alone in a village than a military man, with far less logistical support. For example, the British estimate that the cost of one policeman in a village is much less than that of a soldier.

The UN responsibility for assigning observers to disputed areas might be better met with the use of civilian police. Until now, military personnel have been used, with reliance on small units that drive along borders in jeeps or fly over them in helicopters. According to police specialists, these measures are ineffective if the objective is to check illegal infiltration of personnel and weapons; most illegal traffic today moves through airports and seaports. Civilian police trained in techniques of surveillance and investigation know how to control transportation networks through the use of checkpoints, customs control, passport review, and other specialized types of observation employed in airports, seaports, and major highway intersections. Clearly there can be an important role for civilian as well as military police in UN peacekeeping. Perhaps a civilian police organization with paramilitary training and experience such as the Royal Canadian Mounted Police could make a significant contribution in the future.

Any planning for the future of UN peacekeeping should consider the recent technological advances that might be employed. An important aspect of international control of disputes is an effective early warning system. If the threat to the peace, or the requirement for help, can be ascertained while it is still small, the possibility for effective control increases. There is a need for a more efficient system of information sharing, especially some arrangement to bring warning intelligence to the attention of the Secretary-General. It is not inconceivable that some day the UN will be given access to information obtained from space satellite systems, to electronic intelligence, and to other "black box" information obtained from the gadgets of modern technology.

Psychological resistance today is still probably too strong, but future peacekeepers may be equipped with insurgency and riot control devices such as tranquilizers and gasses that do not maim or kill, but do cause temporary incapacitation. Such agents of persuasion and defense are undoubtedly more humane than conventional weapons. Furthermore, the mere knowledge that the UN units were equipped with them would probably serve as a deterrent. So long as the United Nations concentrates on preventing fighting and maintaining cease-fire, world opinion is more likely to swing behind the employment of such exotic devices.

Among the most important considerations for advancing and perfecting UN peacekeeping are the practical and political implications of participation by Communist states. Some of the Eastern European states have indicated an interest in participating in UN security operations. The time has come to explore this interest, through informal channels, in specific detail. There is need to assess the various political and security problems most likely to emerge; the possible extent of participation in headquarters decisions and in the command and control of field operations; and the capability of available units for specialized duties such as communications, engineering, and medical assistance. The future of peacekeeping will be greatly influenced by the extent to which the Communist states are willing to commit themselves to responsible participation in operations managed by the United Nations.

5

Authorization, Financing, and Direction

For most citizens, even those generally well-informed about foreign affairs, the UN's complex internal politics, procedures, and issues have always seemed somewhat mysterious and distant. Not surprisingly, this still is true, but during the past few years—especially after the widely publicized voteless General Assembly in 1964—one definite public impression emerged: the United Nations was "in a crisis." Its broad outlines became tediously familiar. Budgetary deficits accompanied the refusal of the Soviet Union, France, and other states to pay for certain past peacekeeping operations. Fundamental disagreements persisted among the great powers over the scope of the UN's future peacekeeping authority, over the respective roles of the Security Council and the General Assembly in dispatching peacekeeping missions, over methods of financing future operations, and over the extent of the Secretary-General's executive responsibility for managing and directing peacekeepers in the field.

The public was regularly fed with pessimistic forecasts. Shortly after the February, 1965, adjournment of the Assembly, the *New York Times* headlined that a "UN Crisis Panel of 33" had been formed to resolve the critical issues. One month later, on March 14, Professor Hans J. Morgenthau gave this blunt and unequivocal assessment in the *New York Times Magazine:* ". . . the Security Council is powerless, the General Assembly is powerless, the Secretary-General is powerless. The United Nations has ceased to be an effective international organization."

The "Crisis Panel" (known in UN parlance as the Special Committee on Peacekeeping Operations) reported in June, 1965. All members of the Committee, including the United States and the Soviet Union, agreed that the forthcoming session of the Assembly should function normally; but no significant changes had occurred in the impasse over constitutional and financial issues.

Then, in mid-1965, the United Nations celebrated its twentieth anniversary, amidst feelings that the occasion was, beneath the surface, an elegy rather than a reaffirmation. In an introduction to its July 24 anniversary issue devoted to the UN, the *Saturday Review* editorialized: "The United Nations' twentieth anniversary has come and gone, and nothing happened at the observances in San Francisco to lessen the crisis of the world organization."

In August, after the US dropped its insistence on the enforcement of Article 19, the Special Committee adjourned and the 1965 Assembly debated new proposals for guidelines governing the authorization and financing of future peacekeeping operations. The Assembly closed out its year by acknowledging that none of the proposals was generally acceptable and by remanding them to the Special Committee for further "careful consideration." Again, press comments reflected gloom. On January 8, 1966, the *Economist* referred to the Assembly's "depressingly general unwillingness even to face these hard facts" of peacekeeping problems, and prophesied a "bleak new year for the United Nations." One day later, Drew Middleton, chief UN correspondent for the *New York Times*, titled an interpretive article, "The UN Tries Hard, But—."

The Special Committee met periodically during the next nine months and its Chairman told the 1966 Assembly that he "had endeavored to reconcile the different views held by Member States, but it was not possible to achieve this." There was, the *New York Times* reported on September 14, "no accord on cost formula or authorization." On the following day, the Secretary-General in the *Introduction* to his *Annual Report* said: ". . . I can only reiterate the hope that the General Assembly at its twenty-first session will devote its most serious and determined attention to the problem of peacekeeping, with a view to finding a solution to both its constitutional and its financial problems." Despite a great deal of attention, these problems were unsolved when the Assembly adjourned late in December and remained so after the special session in April and May of 1967.

Pollsters have not yet tried to report and analyze the public reaction to the malaise at the United Nations from 1964–1967. It seems fair to speculate that the residue of these years is a widespread sense that there has been no progress whatsoever, no accommodation that would restore the organization's potency as a peacekeeping agent, no agreed-upon procedures that would permit reliable undertaking of peacekeeping operations—in short, a sense of no movement away from the rigid and incompatible positions that provoked the crisis in the first place. What is important now is to separate fact from myth. As is true with most generalizations about complex and subtle processes, the public view of "the crisis" is only partly accurate.

Modest but significant progress has occurred since 1964. More is known now about the real limitations, and capabilities, of the UN for authorizing and financing peacekeeping operations. More is known about the views of a wide range of member states concerning these issues. More is known about the conditions under which the Secretary-General can function as an effective executive. This knowledge is not just of academic interest; it is important because, with it, none of the great powers is likely to provoke further crises or mistrust by pushing the organization too far or by circumscribing its powers unduly.

The current balance sheet cannot be constructed simply on the basis of the positions of principle held by the main actors, notably the United States, the Soviet Union, and France. These are only partial indicators. They need to be supplemented by evidence of what these states, irrespective of their convictions in principle, have encouraged and permitted the organization to do, especially during the past several years when new peacekeeping action was required in Cyprus, in Kashmir, and on the India-Pakistan border.

Authorization

Stripped of complicated jargon, the "authorization issue" can be formulated as a single question: Which organ of the United Nations—the Security Council or the General Assembly—is empowered to make the final decision to send a peacekeeping mission to a trouble spot? No clear answer is found in the Charter, mainly because the concept and function of peacekeeping forces, as recognized by the majority of UN member states and as used in this book, were not fully foreseen by the drafters of the Charter.

Several articles of the Charter have become lynchpins of the various constitutional and legal arguments on the authorization issue. Article 24, paragraph 1, confers on the Security Council "primary responsibility" for the maintenance of international peace and security. Article 11, paragraph 2, permits the General Assembly "to discuss any questions relating to the maintenance of international peace and security" and to "make recommendations with regard to any such questions." The final sentence in that paragraph states that when "action" is necessary the matter shall be referred to the Security Council. Other articles grant the Assembly power to make recommendations "on any questions or matters within the scope of the Charter" and to recommend measures "for the peaceful adjustment of any situation likely" to impair friendly relations among nations.

Legal interpretations of these and related articles, plus national political perspectives on the outcomes of past peacekeeping operations and on the desirable scope of future ones, buttress and motivate the positions of principle adhered to by the major powers. All the supporting arguments were fully articulated at various times since 1964.

For the Soviet Union, the "primary responsibility" language of Article 24 is tantamount to "exclusive responsibility." In May, 1965, Soviet Ambassador Fedorenko declared: "The essence of that primary responsibility is that the Security Council has sole power under the Charter to decide all questions concerned with taking action for the maintenance of international peace and security, which includes operations using United Nations armed forces." With this as a basic proposition, the Soviets reject any distinction between peacekeeping forces and enforcement or sanctions forces. All units of a military character, the argument goes, whether performing pacifying and supervision functions, observation duties, or enforcement action against a state, can be authorized only by the Security Council, and therefore are subject to the veto. The General Assembly may only discuss and recommend concerning matters relating to peace and security. The Charter requirement in Article 11 that all questions on which "action" is necessary be referred to the Security Council is relied on by the Soviets in support of their position, for they contend that "action" means the dispatch of anything from a small group of military observers to a massive force such as was sent to the Congo.

The United States concedes exclusive powers to the Security Council in all matters relating to mandatory enforcement actions against a state (i.e., steps taken under Chapter VII of the Charter). The US delegate in the special peacekeeping committee said in June, 1965, that "the Security Council should, as it had normally done in the past, authorize future peacekeeping operations. However, the General Assembly should assume that responsibility in appropriate cases whenever enforcement measures were not involved. As Dag Hammarskjold had stated in 1957, enforcement action by the United Nations under Chapter VII of the Charter continued to be reserved to the Security Council. . . ." Beyond this, the positions of the superpowers are almost completely at variance. The central issue is whether the General Assembly may authorize peacekeeping operations when the Security Council is prevented from doing so by the veto. The US answer is affirmative: the Assembly possesses a "residual" power to authorize peacekeeping operations—a power that is no less extensive than that of the Security Council on peacekeeping matters. For the US the word "action" in Article 11 means *only* enforcement action (an interpretation that has been supported by the International Court of Justice). Thus, the Assembly need not necessarily refer proposals for peacekeeping operations to the Security Council for authorization.

Somewhere in between lies the French position. The French contend that forces, whether military or not and regardless of their size, may be authorized by the Assembly only if they are restricted to the performance of observation, supervision, or inquiry functions. Presumably the French view would mean that the Cyprus force, for example, which carries out quasi-military duties such as assisting in maintaining law and order and preserving the cease-fire, could never have been authorized by the General Assembly.

Other member states have offered slightly different versions of these major positions; legal hairs have been split; Charter terminology has been defined and redefined; suggestions have even been made for amending the Charter by inserting new articles governing peacekeeping operations. Ironically, however, as the conflicting viewpoints have hardened, the urgency of the need to settle this issue and to reach formal agreement has diminished sharply. The authorization issue has become less critical—and rightly so, because politically the costs of trying to hammer out precise and agreed lines of authority for the Assembly and the Security Council far outweigh any gains that could possibly accrue to the United Nations.

In the spring of 1966, in off-the-record conversations, this conviction was expressed repeatedly by key UN delegations, Western, Communist, and Third World. In May, Swedish Ambassador Astrom stated publicly in the Special Committee on Peacekeeping Operations what nearly everyone had been saying privately for some time. The Committee, he said, should apply a "double test in deciding which areas of disagreement to tackle: First we should attempt to establish whether progress in a particular field is of real and immediate importance to preserve the capability of the United Nations to act efficiently for the maintenance of peace. Second, we should try to determine whether such progress is within the realm of reasonable hopes of attainment." On the basis of these criteria of desirability and feasibility, he advised the Committee "to put aside for the time being the problem of the relative competence of the Security Council and the General Assembly" because there is "no reason" to believe that differing views could be reconciled and because it is unclear whether any useful purpose would be served by laying down, in advance, more specific rules governing the problems of competence. Justifications for Ambassador Astrom's conclusion were not explicit in his speech to the Committee; they deserve further explanation and evaluation.

In the autumn of 1965, an unsuccessful effort was made by Ireland, with the support of seven African, Asian, and Latin American states, to get Assembly approval for a resolution recognizing its residual peacekeeping authority. Responses to the proposal were no surprise. The major powers had not changed their positions, and it was also clear that none of them was willing to make a serious attempt to force acceptance of its views by the others. The Soviets and the French know well that the majority of the member states definitely will not accept any express revocation of the Assembly's peacekeeping authority; the United States knows equally well that the same majority will not acquiesce in any attempt, reminiscent of US Article 19 tactics, to force express confirmation of that authority on a reluctant minority.

These attitudes were confirmed emphatically during the 1966 session of the Assembly. Canada submitted a major peacekeeping plan recognizing, among other things, "that if the Security Council is unable to adopt decisions, the General Assembly, which bears its share of responsibility in maintaining international peace and security, may consider the matter in accordance with the Charter and make appropriate recommendations. . . ." In committee, where a simple majority assures passage of a resolution, the Canadian proposal had been adopted. But when it was scheduled for a vote in the Assembly, the Soviet Union and France launched an intense lobbying effort to defeat the proposal. The Soviets capped the effort with a strong written statement charging that the draft resolution constituted a violation of the Charter and warning that adoption by the Assembly would be "latent with serious consequences for the United Nations." Largely because of this Communist opposition to the language quoted above, the Assembly adopted a resolution, sponsored by some nineteen nonaligned states, deferring consideration of the Canadian plan until a later date.

The important question, politically, is whether this stand-off of principle genuinely impairs the UN's peacekeeping capabilities. An Eastern European diplomat who has been intimately involved in peacekeeping negotiations for his delegation said privately that he "is not too concerned about the gap" that appears to separate the great powers. "Underneath the positions of principle," he added, "the gap is far narrower than it appears to be" on the surface. Similar comments were made by numerous neutral and Western diplomats. Historical record and recent trends in the peacekeeping field, particularly since the Congo operation, explain this attitude—and suggest that it is politically realistic.

There is, first of all, no evidence that during the past twenty years the United Nations was prevented from initiating any needed peacekeeping action because of disagreement about constitutional or legal principles. Yet, in one or another form, divergent views have been held since the very beginning. True, during the early years Western preponderance in both the Security Council and the Assembly virtually assured this majority that it could have an operation if it wanted one badly enough. (In 1947, for example, when Soviet vetoes obstructed peacekeeping efforts in the Balkans, the question was later dealt with by the Assembly.)

A turning point in the constitutional sphere came in 1950 with the adoption by the Assembly of the Uniting for Peace resolution. Though not a grant of new authority to the Assembly, the resolution embodied various substantive and procedural provisions that would assure and institutionalize the Assembly's power to act when the Security Council is veto-bound. Soviet reactions to the American-inspired maneuver were—and still are—bitterly negative; but six years later when the French and British vetoed Security Council action during the Suez crisis, the Soviets *voted for* a Yugoslav proposal to invoke the Uniting for Peace procedures. It was then left to the Assembly, with the Soviet Union abstaining, to create UNEF. National interests, not constitutional arguments, clearly dictated the abstention.

After Soviet ambitions were frustrated during the Congo operation, the Communists hardened their insistence on Security Council control over all peacekeeping matters. It was generally believed that this meant they were not likely again to permit in practice what they opposed in principle, and that the Suez pattern of Assembly-authorized peacekeeping, with the Soviets abstaining, was no longer possible. Yet this—and more—is precisely what happened in 1962.

In October of that year, UN action had been proposed in connection with a written agreement between Indonesia and the Netherlands concerning the disposition of West New Guinea. The General Assembly had been asked by the parties to accept the agreement and to take steps to implement it, including the creation and dispatch of "a United Nations security force to maintain law and order." Every Communist member of the Assembly cast a "yes" vote for this resolution—even though shortly after, on December 19, a Soviet delegate in a main committee of the Assembly stated categorically that in his country's view "peacekeeping operations could not be undertaken except in pursuance of a decision by the Security Council." Despite such convictions, and despite the Congo experience, the Soviet Union has acted pragmatically, often responsive to the legitimate desires of the Third World constituency in the UN.

Ambassador Astrom's suggestion that the authorization issue be put aside for the time being probably rests too on the recent record of increased Security Council involvement in the peace and security field—a situation preferred by the United States as well as the Soviet Union. The main reason for continuing US insistence on the option of Assembly authority is not so much a conviction that the Assembly ought to be an alternate decision-maker on peacekeeping matters, but rather a belief—probably well founded—that the Assembly option has been a deterrent to the use of capricious, obstructive vetoes in the Security Council. With the West Irian exception, every peacekeeping operation in recent years has been initiated by the Council: Yemen in 1962, Cyprus in 1964, Kashmir and the Indian-Pakistan border observers in 1965. This is likely to be the pattern for most future operations, and it is supported by a growing number of member states, including US allies such as the Netherlands and Australia as well as some neutral states, that believe that any formal resuscitation of Uniting for Peace procedures would jeopardize the fragile peacekeeping consensus that could well exist among the great powers for future Cypruses and Kashmirs.

Financing

Two factors contribute to the persistent apprehension at the United Nations about the financial aspects of peacekeeping. First, the assessments for the UNEF and Congo operations have never been fully paid; second, the methods available for future financing are less reliable than the system of compulsory assessments the United States had hoped to enforce with the Article 19 threat. The central political lesson of the Article 19 crisis is that no state, surely no great power, can be compelled to pay for operations that it disapproves of politically.

THE DEFICIT. The nature of the UN's financial problems can be represented in either of two ways: by calculating the total amount of assessments that member states have failed to pay, or by comparing financial assets and liabilities and arriving at a fairly precise deficit figure. Different conclusions emerge from these two approaches, and understanding why this is so is essential in order to comprehend the real significance of the UN's financial situation.

The Soviet Union and its allies have refused to pay their assessments for UNEF and the Congo operation, as well as certain smaller peacekeeping-related items financed out of the regular UN budget. France has done likewise for the Congo operation costs and for part of the regular budget, and other states have not paid their full shares of some or all of these items. Total unpaid assessments amount to $125.9 million: $82.5 million for the Congo operation, $33.8 million for UNEF, $9.3 million for the regular budget. Of this, the Communist states plus France owe $99.9 million.

This $125.9 million is what the United Nations is owed by member states; but the deficit can be calculated only by subtracting current financial assets from liabilities. The total amount of unpaid assessments is greater than the deficit because expenditures have not been financed solely by assessments. Shortages resulting from assessment arrearages have been offset over the years by periodic emergency financing measures, such as unconditional voluntary contributions, that created no additional financial liability. Thus, the oft-heard assertion that "the UN still is over $100 million in the red" is simply not correct.

The United States, France, the Soviet Union, and eleven other states spent several months in 1966 sorting out the UN's financial affairs. They all agreed that the current deficit was less than one-half the amount of unpaid assessments—how much less depends on whether the US, or the French and Soviets, were making the estimates. The "Committee of 14" compromised and accepted both sets of calculations. To the evident puzzlement of most observers outside the UN, they said the deficit is either as low as $31.9 million (French and Soviet figure) or as high as $53.3 million (US figure).

UN financial assets fall into three broad categories: (1) payments realistically expected from assessments for current and prior years; (2) voluntary contributions received but still unallocated; (3) liquid assets on hand. The Committee members agreed that available assets totalled $55.8 to $60.7 million.

On the liability side of the ledger the Committee listed: (1) repayments owed to a cash-on-hand Working Capital Fund in the UN budget; (2) money owed, mostly to member states, for goods and services provided on a reimbursable basis; (3) repayments to member states who had made voluntary contributions conditional on the understanding that the money would be returned at a future date. The Committee agreed that these items totalled \$96.6–\$97.6 million. It was a fourth liability category, relating to so-called "surplus accounts," that caused the different conclusions.

The term "surplus accounts" in UN budgetary language refers to the excess of funds appropriated over actual expenditures. When this excess shows on the books, member states are usually given credits against future assessments in an amount equal to their assessed proportion of the surplus funds. The United States insists that a surplus exists in both the UNEF and Congo accounts because the total of all assessments for these operations, if they had been paid, plus the total of the UN bonds used to cover the Congo operation and UNEF shortfalls would have produced an amount in excess of expenditures. Even though the surplus is a theoretical one, its existence must necessarily be asserted if the United States is to be consistent with its position that these assessments and bonds for UNEF and the Congo operation were legally binding.

The French and Soviets, because they reject the legality of the two operations, deny the budgetary relevance of the extraordinary measures used to finance them, and maintain that the two accounts show shortages rather than surpluses. In either case it is worth noting that, for most of the states to whom credits might be due, the amount concerned would be comparatively trivial: \$15.5 million in the two surplus accounts would have to be divided proportionately among fifty-one member states that paid their full assessments for UNEF and the Congo operation and thirty-nine others that have made partial payment of their assessments.

It is now clear that most other members of the "Committee of 14" are not insisting that the Soviet Union and France make voluntary contributions equal to the amount of their unpaid assessments to erase the debt. Explicit in the Committee's report is the conclusion that voluntary contributions totalling \$31.9–\$53.3 million (the deficit estimates) would clear the books to everyone's satisfaction, though the unpaid assessments of the Communist states and France total nearly $100 million.

During the early months of 1967, indications were that the Soviets and the French would tender voluntary contributions, presumably in proportion to the lower deficit figures. Without these contributions, the deficit would have to be alleviated by other voluntary contributions, which could take the form of outright payments or, for some states, reductions of long-standing national claims for reimbursements from the UN. These claims constitute the bulk of the organization's unliquidated obligations.

FUTURE FINANCING. In attempting to devise reliable financing methods for future operations, it must be recognized that assessed contributions are no longer a viable source of peacekeeping funds. No alternative will be as neat and, ostensibly at least, as fool-proof as the assessment system; but a variety of nonmandatory financing techniques are available. Skillful and imaginative use of them can produce flexible patterns of financing that will give needed credibility to the principle of collective financial responsibility and, most important of all, take into account the essentially political nature of peacekeeping financing.

Four financing methods have survived and are currently being used. Others have been suggested during recent years. The first, and simplest, is financing on what might be called a "benefits-received" principle; that is, the states that benefit directly from the presence of peacekeeping forces pay for their maintenance. Two recent operations have been funded in this way by agreement of the parties concerned, and it appears generally recognized that this method will be adequate for some future operations that are relatively modest in size, cost, and duration. When the governments of Saudi Arabia and the UAR agreed in 1963 to an observation mission that remained in Yemen for a little over a year, they also agreed to defray in equally divided shares the mission's operating costs, estimated at $1.8 million. One year earlier, the Netherlands and Indonesia similarly shared the costs for the seven-month peacekeeping operation in West Irian, estimated at $20 million.

A second basic financing method was used for the first time in the Cyprus operation. Created in March, 1964, the Cyprus force, under the terms of the Security Council's enabling resolution, is financed entirely by voluntary contributions from member states. For operations from its inception to June, 1967, the force is expected to cost $69.7 million. As of the beginning of May, 1967, forty-seven governments have pledged a total of $63 million. Assuming further pledges by the end of the year, the operation is running at a deficit of something like $4–5 million—an improvement over 1965, when the deficit was about $10 million. In any event, the Cyprus operation is not likely to fail for lack of money. Its continuation is so clearly in the interests of most member states that, in the words of one Scandinavian diplomat, it is unthinkable that the force would be discontinued "just because of a few million dollars."

The third financing technique, in common use before the financial crisis provoked by UNEF and the Congo operation, is the funding of operations out of the regular budget—if necessary by shifting available resources from one budget category to another. It too is likely to be an acceptable method for modest financing in the future. Recent operations on the borders of Israel, on the India-Pakistan border, and in Kashmir have been financed in this way; the latter two provide a good illustration of how operations are financed out of the regular budget.

Each fiscal year the General Assembly authorizes in the regular budget the equivalent of a "contingency fund" empowering the Secretary-General to incur obligations not provided for in the regular budget. Up to $2 million of this fund may be used to cover expenses of any operation that is certified by the Secretary-General as relating to the maintenance of peace and security. If the amount needed by the Secretary-General to implement a decision of the Security Council is more than $2 million, but not more than $10 million, he must seek prior approval for using the fund from a small Advisory Committee that oversees interim expenditures.

After hostilities broke out in 1965 between India and Pakistan, the UN took two steps: it expanded the force of military observers that had been operating in Kashmir since 1950 (UN Military Observer Group in India and Pakistan) from 43 to 102, including appropriate increases in support facilities; and it established a second observation group (UN India-Pakistan Observation Mission) of 96 observers to patrol the cease-fire along the India-Pakistan border outside Kashmir. The strengthening of UNMOGIP was financed out of the contingency fund until the General Assembly authorized the necessary funds to be taken from the regular budget. Because UNIPOM was an entirely new mission, the Secretary-General could not rely on an existing budget category or on a routine method of supplementary financing. Therefore, the funding technique was somewhat different. In 1965, UNIPOM costs were financed initially out of the 1965 contingency fund. Similarly, the 1966 fund was used to finance 1966 costs until the mission was terminated in March of that year. Both amounts were covered later each year by a bookkeeping technique whereby the contingency fund is replenished by credits available from other sections of the regular budget.

The fourth financing method used represents an attempt to find a middle ground between mandatory and wholly voluntary payments for major operations—in this case, UNEF. This so-called "apportionment" system is essentially a cost-sharing device that *anticipates* nonpayment by those states that object to the force on political grounds. UNEF expenditures from 1965 on were financed on this assumption. Total estimated costs for 1967, for example, were $14 million. A little over 5 percent of this total was apportioned on a "capacity-to-pay" principle among the large majority of states designated in the resolution as "economically less developed"; the remaining 95 percent was distributed among twenty-six developed states. The latter group, additionally, was apportioned 25 percent of their base contribution—the amount necessary to compensate for expected shortfall.

Efforts to find agreed procedures for financing future peacekeeping operations, especially those involving relatively large expenditures, have centered on discussions of two plans devised recently, one by Ireland, the other by Canada. The financial provisions of the Irish plan, first submitted during the 1965 Assembly, provoked considerable controversy, revealing the inherent difficulty of trying, with one hand, to retain at least a semblance of the principle of collective financial responsibility while trying, with the other, to acknowledge that states can no longer be compelled to pay for what they consider politically undesirable peacekeeping operations (although this balance, in effect, was being maintained in the UNEF financing arrangements).

The Irish plan was designed for use in financing operations authorized either by the Assembly or the Security Council. Its principal features were: a provision enabling any permanent member of the Security Council who does not vote for an operation to "opt out" of all financial responsibility; and a cost-sharing formula according to which 5 percent of an operation would be paid by developing states, 25 percent by developed states not permanent members of the Security Council, and 70 percent by the permanent members voting for the operation, with the proviso that no single permanent member be expected to bear more than 50 percent of the total costs.

The Irish plan failed to gain general support. The authorizing arrangements in the plan were opposed by the Communist countries and others that object to the Uniting for Peace procedures. Also, the large majority of member states, while recognizing in principle that special responsibility for peacekeeping falls on the great powers, are not willing to institutionalize a financing system that confers the "opting out" privilege only on the permanent members of the Security Council: if the privilege is to be applicable at all, it should be nondiscriminatory among all states.

Mindful of the objections to the Irish financing plan, leading members of the Special Committee on Peacekeeping Operations publicly made proposals in 1966 that would give all states the prerogative of "opting out" of financial responsibility, confirming the political inevitability of reliance on essentially voluntary financing, at least when operations of a fairly major scale are involved. When the 1966 Assembly convened, Canada included in its peacekeeping plan a clause recognizing "that various methods of financing peacekeeping operations may be considered" for use in the future. Mandatory assessments were not among the methods listed by the Canadians, though the plan did suggest that for any future operation financed by the apportionment method, a special budgetary scale should be used as a guideline for member states' payments. Presumably this scale, which assigns 5 percent of total costs to economically less developed states and the remainder to all other states, would allow for the "opting out" privilege of any state that chooses not to pay its share of an operation's costs, and could be used to finance operations authorized either by the Assembly or by the Security Council. As indicated earlier in this chapter, the Assembly refused to act on any aspect of the Canadian proposal. It seems fairly certain, however, that any formal arrangement for future financing will be based on the essential features of the Canadian cost-sharing plan.

THE EFFECT OF VOLUNTARISM ON UNITED STATES FINANCING TECHNIQUES. The August, 1965, US "reservation" that it would claim the right to refuse payment for undesirable UN operations has been reflected in changed procedures within the US government for requesting and appropriating contributions to international peacekeeping operations.

A high degree of flexibility now exists among the various categories of funds from which the State Department can draw in order to meet US financial obligations for peacekeeping. Contributions to international organizations are drawn from three sources: the annual budget of the State Department, Chapter III of the Foreign Assistance Act (titled "Voluntary Contributions to International Organizations"), and the Contingency Fund of the Foreign Assistance Act. All funds for the payment of US assessments to the regular budget of the UN come out of the State Department's annual budget. The familiar 33⅓ percent ceiling—i.e., the Congressional limitation imposed in 1952 to the effect that no representative of the United States may accept an assessed obligation of more than 33⅓ percent of the annual budget for any international organization—applies to funds allocated from the State Department's budget. Voluntary contributions to activities outside the UN's regular assessed budget are requested from Chapter III of the Foreign Aid funds if the amount and object of the proposed expenditures can be identified in advance of Congressional authorization action. If the voluntary expenditures are unforeseen, the amounts can later be taken from the Contingency Fund that is part of the annual Foreign Assistance Act. The 33⅓ percent ceiling does not apply to voluntary contributions.

All of these categories are being used in fiscal 1967 to finance US shares of UN peacekeeping costs. To those operations that are still financed from the UN's regular budget, such as the observer missions in Kashmir and in Palestine, the United States contributes 31.9 percent of the total, the same proportion as the overall US contribution to the UN's regular budget.

Until very recently, the US share of UNEF costs was paid out of both the State Department's budget and Chapter III—the former to cover the assessed portion, the latter to cover voluntary contributions designed to offset expected shortfalls. After the General Assembly developed the "apportionment" device for financing UNEF, the United States changed its internal procedures accordingly. On the Assembly vote, the US declared that, though it supported the new device, it would be forced to abstain because the amount apportioned to it exceeded 33⅓ percent of the total. It was, in fact, approximately 37 percent of 1966 expenditures. The entire amount is now taken out of the funds for voluntary contributions in Chapter III. This means, in effect, that so long as the UN "apportions" rather than "assesses" peacekeeping costs, the US is free to consider this a contribution that is not limited to 33⅓ percent. Confirming this, Assistant Secretary of State for International Organization Affairs Joseph Sisco told Congress: "While some members of the UN will interpret this resolution for UNEF for $15 million next year as a binding mandatory assessment, from our point of view, we essentially construe it as a voluntary contribution." No member of Congress challenged this interpretation.

The other large-scale peacekeeping operation, the Cyprus force, has always been paid for out of either Chapter III or the Contingency Fund in an amount approximating 40.4 percent of the total.

Thus no major peacekeeping operation is now being financed by assessed contributions. It is clear that the 33⅓ percent limitation has never been and is not likely to be a controlling factor in the amount the United States can pay for UN peacekeeping. Even before recent changes, US assessed and voluntary contributions totalled for the Congo operation slightly less than 42 percent, and for UNEF almost 43 percent over ten years.

The Secretary-General and Executive Responsibility

Understanding the flexibility available in authorization procedures and in UN and US financing techniques provides an important background for an examination of the most critical internal issue at the United Nations: the extent of the Secretary-General's responsibility. Whether and how the authorization powers of the UN bodies are utilized and their implementation is paid for depends, in large part, on his skill and sensitivity.

Brian Urquhart, a high-level Secretariat official who has been closely associated with policy-making for UN peacekeeping during the terms of the last two Secretaries-General, said in a speech in 1965 that at the UN, "the number of things which are purportedly not acceptable but which have been done and are constantly being done is remarkable. One is the initiative and responsibility given to the Secretary-General and the extraordinary increase of confidence between him and the Member Governments." The increasing political role of the Secretary-General is certainly the most significant development in recent UN history. However, realistic and cautious expectations about the further expansion of his role need also be kept in mind, for his capabilities are by no means open-ended. When the Secretary-General and the Secretariat act, Urquhart continued, "our authority is extremely limited, and we have to be based very securely when we do anything because if we are not, first we get no results, and secondly we lose the support of the Governments, without which we cannot operate at all." The balance is delicate, but the powers of the Secretary-General are neither as extensive as the "one-worlders" would like nor as narrow as some critics suggest.

In September, 1966, when Soviet Ambassador Fedorenko emphatically reiterated the Soviet Union's views on the prerogatives of the Security Council in peace and security matters, he outlined by implication the areas of responsibility that his government insists should be denied to the Secretary-General. "Falling explicitly within the specific competence of the Security Council," he said, "are found questions such as the task and function of the armed forces, their numbers and composition, their command structure, the duration of their service in the field, the direction of such operations, and the mode of financing the necessary expenditures. No one else—no other organ, no person, no official of the United Nations—is empowered to carry out such actions in measures relating to the use of armed forces." The French, while not articulating demands as unequivocal as these, also couple their preference for paramountcy of the Security Council in peacekeeping decisions with a narrow conception of the authority of the Secretary-General.

Operating responsibilities for the Secretary-General are invariably a part of every peacekeeping arrangement authorized by one or another body of the UN. No group of states wishes to deny him a role in the management of an operation. Rather, the differences of opinion relate to whether he is to function as purely an administrative officer or as a relatively independent agent within the limits set by the broad guidelines laid down by the authorizing body. Clearly, these are not mutually exclusive categories, for by the nature of his office the Secretary-General nearly always acts, in one observer's words, as a "political administrator."

The Soviet insistence on a strict and narrow construction of the Secretary-General's responsibilities is predicated not so much on any dissatisfaction with the performance of the incumbent Secretary-General, U Thant, as it is on a concern for the institution of the Secretary-General. An Eastern European diplomat said privately that his government opposes "independent, executive" action because of the precedent it might set, because "we do not know who will be occupying that position after U Thant and we do not know how he will be inclined to conduct himself." Herein lies the heart of the issue. Seen as a product of the Soviet bloc's disaffection with the former Secretary-General, this attitude is understandable, even if frustratingly stubborn and abstract in light of the record of U Thant.

One suspects, and recent experience indicates, that the Soviets are forced by circumstances to view the role of the Secretary-General—now and in the future—far more constructively than their speeches suggest. One Third World ambassador said privately that he does not believe that the Soviet Union's public utterances on the subject ought to be taken as "givens" or "constants." He added that Soviet diplomats know quite well what he means when he tells them: "If you want to prevent the misuse of the United Nations, you have no choice but to trust the Secretary-General. Your efforts, therefore, must be directed at guaranteeing that he can be trusted and at building mutual trust from within the organization." The Soviets have shown considerable trust for the actions of the incumbent. They know that the next Secretary-General will have to be initially acceptable to themselves as well as to the other great powers. They know that the next office holder could hardly fail to learn the lessons left to him by U Thant. They know that in view of the hard and rapid decision-making required for peacekeeping, the organization could not function at all without initiatives on the part of the Secretary-General and his staff.

Have they, particularly in the last several years, acted accordingly? The answer must be a qualified "yes." The question is not whether the Soviets are willing now to allow the Secretary-General to function as freely as most members of the UN would like, but whether they are moving in that direction. There is evidence that they are. Recalling the words of Ambassador Fedorenko quoted earlier, it is revealing to examine in some detail what the public record shows concerning the extent to which they have permitted relatively independent action.

In the West Irian operation, the General Assembly resolution empowered the Secretary-General: to appoint a United Nations Administrator for the mission; to provide such security forces as the Administrator deemed necessary; to receive the reports of the Administrator and to exercise his discretion about whether to submit his own reports to the General Assembly or to Member States. The Soviets voted for the resolution.

The issue of the Secretary-General's competence was raised in connection with the Security Council's authorization of the Cyprus force. The enabling resolution recommended that "The composition and size of the force shall be established by the Secretary-General, in consultation with the Governments of Cyprus, Greece, Turkey and the United Kingdom. The commander of the force shall be appointed by the Secretary-General and report to him." The details of this resolution were, of course, fully discussed by all the great powers prior to the meeting of the Security Council. So it was no surprise to anyone that in a separate vote on the above portions of the text the Soviet Union, Czechoslovakia, and France registered their objections in principle by abstaining. But there was a unanimous "yes" vote on the resolution as a whole. The French delegate merely remarked about the critical paragraph that he considered the Council to be "going very far indeed in the direction of the delegation of powers to grant them in this way to a single individual."

The votes tell part of the story, and the attitudes of the Soviets —and the French—during the conduct of the Cyprus operation tell the rest. As indicated in Chapter 2, the great powers are all agreed that the Secretary-General and his staff in Cyprus have been impartial and also that they have acted to the positive satisfaction of all great powers. There is no evidence that the Secretary-General was unable to function effectively because of attempts to limit his freedom. All in all, when the political consensus for effective peacekeeping exists, as it surely does in the case of Cyprus, a Soviet or a French abstention on one paragraph of a resolution is a very small price to pay for the differences in opinion over the role of the Secretary-General.

Most revealing of Soviet permissiveness is the performance of the Secretary-General in the two operations undertaken on the Indian subcontinent during 1965 and 1966. In each case the authority that the great powers apparently allowed him to exercise was extraordinary under the circumstances. On September 6, 1965, two days after it had called for a cease-fire, the Security Council authorized action by unanimously adopting an enabling resolution requesting the Secretary-General "to take all measures possible to strengthen the United Nations Military Observer Group in India and Pakistan (UNMOGIP)." Without further instructions from the Council, U Thant proceeded to ask various governments for the necessary personnel, transport facilities, and the like in numbers that he thought necessary, to be financed in a manner determined by him.

On September 20, the Council, with affirmative votes from the United States, the Soviet Union, and France, requested the Secretary-General "to provide the necessary assistance to ensure supervision of the cease-fire and withdrawal of all armed personnel." In response the Secretary-General reported three days later: "I have decided to organize the Observers whose function it is to supervise the cease-fire and withdrawals as an organization separate from UNMOGIP, entitled United Nations India-Pakistan Observation Mission (UNIPOM)." In other words, the Secretary-General created a new peacekeeping mission, gave it a commander, resources, and money—all within only the very broadest of mandates from the Security Council.

Stories circulated in the press during October, 1965—and US officials indicated privately—that Soviet behavior behind the scenes consisted of regular and insistent efforts to limit the Secretary-General's freedom of action. Reportedly both Ambassador Fedorenko of the USSR and Ambassador Seydoux of France took the position that they would not even acquiesce in any future peacekeeping if the Security Council did not approve in advance the composition, commander, and equipment of the force, as well as the means of financing. Nonetheless, it was not until a month later that Ambassador Fedorenko raised the authority issue in the Council. "We have a question in our minds," he said, "which is of significance *in terms of principle* [emphasis added]. The Soviet delegation deems it essential to draw the attention of the Security Council to the fact that the actions undertaken by the Secretary-General in the question of the United Nations observers in India and Pakistan . . . depart from the provisions of the United Nations Charter, in accordance with which only the Security Council is competent to adopt appropriate measures on concrete questions connected with observers of the United Nations. . . ."

The UNIPOM operation raises some interesting points about the frequently advanced suggestion that the mandates from authorizing bodies must be made more explicit and detailed. Experience with UNIPOM and with the Cyprus force suggests, instead, that neither mission would have been launched rapidly enough if the Council had become bogged down in formulating a precise mandate.

The decisions on concrete questions are the ones the Secretary-General must and can make. What is needed to implement them is the dedication of the peacekeeping nations and the equally important efforts of the staff members in the Secretariat, who invariably are given operating responsibilities in all aspects of peacekeeping.

It is accurately said that there are no full-time peacekeepers in the Secretariat. Among the vast personnel roster of Secretariat employees, there is only one person with the word "peacekeeping" in his official title. This statistic, however, shrouds a great deal of middle and lower level peacekeeping-related activity by Secretariat officials, both at headquarters and in the field. In the field alone, 400 to 500 international civil servants are assigned to the various current peacekeeping operations, serving as political, legal, administrative, and information officers; radio operators and technicians; vehicle mechanics; secretaries; and general duty personnel.

Nonetheless, peacekeeping still is a part-time art at the United

Nations; it is still in embryonic stages; it is still a patchwork of *ad hoc* procedures. Perhaps the single most important lesson in this examination of the issues is that the interests of all states will be served—and most of them know it—if every effort is made to exploit the *ad hoc* approach to the limits of available political consensus. Demonstrably, such exploitation is possible, and the limits have not yet been reached.

Lincoln Bloomfield wisely said in his April, 1966, *Foreign Affairs* article: "... on the assumption that UN peacekeeping will be invoked in the future, yet will continue to rest on a fragmented political foundation, common sense favors arrangements that do not put the existence of the organization at stake each time such a task must be undertaken."

6

Prospects for the Future

The science of weapons and war has made us all . . . one world and one human race, with one common destiny. In such a world absolute sovereignty no longer assures us of absolute security. The convictions of peace must pull abreast and then ahead of the inventions of war. The United Nations, building on its successes and learning from its failures, must be developed into a genuine world security system.

PRESIDENT JOHN F. KENNEDY, SEPTEMBER 20, 1963

The trouble is that we have been lost in a semantic jungle for too long. We have come to identify "security" with exclusively military phenomena; and most particularly military hardware. . . .

A nation can reach the point at which it does not buy more security for itself simply by buying more military hardware—we are at that point.

The decisive factor for a powerful nation—already adequately armed—is the character of its relationships with the world.

SECRETARY OF DEFENSE ROBERT MCNAMARA, MAY 18, 1966

Compared to all other nations, the United States is more than adequately armed, but this vast arsenal, never even approximated in history, does not guarantee the peace—neither do military alliances such as NATO, SEATO, CENTO, and ANZUS, nor forty-two defense treaties with individual governments. These arrangements, all linked with US military power, have helped to contain the Cold War and deter nuclear hot war. Yet there have been 164 internationally significant outbreaks of violence in the last eight years. According to Secretary of Defense McNamara, the number of incidents has increased each year, from 34 in 1958 to 58 in 1965. Most of these have occurred in the Third World states of Asia, Africa, Latin America, and the Middle East—particularly in the areas of the power vacuum remaining after the demise of European colonialism.

Undoubtedly there will continue to be brushfires each year, ignited by struggles for power within governments, insurgencies and counter-insurgencies, external subversion, racial tension, religious conflict, and border disputes. As in the past, most of these will be resolved by the action of individual governments, or by coups d'état, or by some form of negotiation, conciliation, mediation, or arbitration. But some of them will get out of control and will require an international fire brigade. The United States alone cannot take on this responsibility throughout the world, and the alternatives to US power are very slim.

The United Nations is the principal source of peacekeeping know-how, experience, and authority, and, despite its imperfections, it provides a feasible alternative in some circumstances to US power. The UN has demonstrated on several occasions a capacity to conduct effective peacekeeping operations with military personnel in disputes where US forces would not have been welcome, and where their unilateral interposition would probably have had disastrous consequences for the United States.

In 1962, in an address that still reflects the thinking of an influential segment of US opinion, Senator Henry M. Jackson, Democrat from the State of Washington and Chairman of the Subcommittee on National Security and International Operations, spoke to the National Press Club on the subject, "The US in the UN: An Independent Audit." He said: "The United Nations is not, and was never intended to be, a substitute for our own leaders as makers and movers of American policy. The shoulders of the Secretary-General were never expected to carry the burdens of the President or the Secretary of State. But do we sometimes act as though we could somehow subcontract to the UN the responsibility for national decision-making?" Senator Jackson, one of the most influential members of the Senate in national security affairs, was right then and would be right today in asserting that the UN cannot be a substitute for our own leaders as makers of US policy.

The point is, rather, that action through the United Nations is one of the foreign policy options available to the President. The UN can and should be a substitute for US military involvement in certain circumstances. When that happens the Secretary-General does indeed carry some of the burdens that might otherwise be carried by the President and the Secretary of State. The United States, for obvious reasons, gives first priority to its own power, but even though the UN may continue to be only a small part of US security policy thinking, there are good reasons for giving more attention to the UN alternative and for strengthening its capacity to act.

Speaking at Harvard in June, 1963, Secretary-General U Thant said: "The idea that conventional military methods or, to put it bluntly, war—can be used by or on behalf of the United Nations to counter aggression and secure the peace, seems now to be rather impractical." He explained that peacekeeping operations should not be confused with the use of force to counter aggression as provided for in Chapter VII of the Charter and said peacekeeping units "are essentially peace and not fighting forces and they operate only with the consent of the parties directly concerned."

The Soviets have intentionally confused peacekeeping forces with fighting forces. In part, this is because they genuinely fear that a peacekeeping force will be used as a fighting force—as in the Katanga phase of the Congo operation. But more important is their desire to have some control over the management of future operations, which they hope to ensure by insisting that all

UN forces, regardless of their purpose, be directed through the Security Council.

As U Thant indicates, it does not seem practical to expect the United Nations to wage war again, as it did in Korea, to carry out a decision. However, it would not be prudent to rule out the possibility altogether. The authority does exist in the Charter even though contemporary world politics make its use seem almost out of the question. It is remotely conceivable, for example, that the Soviet Union and the United States would some day authorize a UN force to secure the independence of the mandated territory of South West Africa, and thus to prevent South Africa from applying the abhorrent policy of apartheid. It is also possible, though even more unlikely, that a UN force might be authorized in a limited war situation, particularly if Communist China were supporting the aggresson. If the Security Council ever again authorizes a sanctions force the combat units might have to be provided by the major powers, probably the superpowers, and this could happen only if both superpowers agreed to participate. Most of the neutral or neutralist nations that have participated in peacekeeping operations probably would not take part in any combat force.

For the foreseeable future it would be wiser to pursue the present course of differentiating sharply between peacekeeping and enforcement operations. Policy-makers should think of the United Nations as the principal source of peacekeeping, and should, usually, look elsewhere when substantial military force is required. Furthermore, the Secretary-General and his Secretariat should be regarded as the administrative center for implementing such peacekeeping assignments as the UN may approve. The Soviets will undoubtedly continue to insist that the authority of the Secretary-General be under strict Security Council control. Though the Soviet official position is categorically at odds with a strong discretionary role for the Secretary-General, the record shows that their votes and their action have often supported peacekeeping operations directed by the Secretary-General, even though they have not contributed to the financing.

There are certain overriding political considerations that make UN peacekeeping feasible even in the face of the Vietnam gulf between the superpowers. Though their motivations may differ, the Soviet Union and the United States may support UN peacekeeping to thwart Communist Chinese ambitions, as in the recent India-Pakistan dispute. The Soviets are inclined, also, to go along with UN action supported by a large Afro-Asian consensus, as was the case in the Congo. In spite of initial reluctance, they supported UN involvement in Cyprus because they much preferred that alternative to NATO. It is also possible that they will support UN action in some instances when they are persuaded that the alternative would be a unilateral US move. This last consideration cuts both ways as far as Soviet policy options are concerned because in some instances they will hope for some degree of influence over the course of a particular dispute, but in others they would prefer to see unilateral US intervention, fully aware of the damaging repercussions such intervention usually has for any nation.

Both the United States and the Soviet Union are aware that under the cloak of collective responsibility UN peacekeeping permits action without committing the vital interests of either great power. UN operations can extinguish brushfires without great-power confrontation. The United Nations provides a diplomatic center where a third party—either the Secretary-General, a single nation, or a group of nations—can originate a proposal for action that may be acceptable to the US and USSR, but could not possibly have been initiated through direct Washington-Moscow channels. The UN is a forum where the superpowers can collaborate with minimum loss of face and therefore less danger of adverse domestic political repercussions.

The United Nations and Vietnam

Because the United Nations was founded primarily to maintain peace, there has been clamor, particularly in the United States, to involve the organization in the Vietnam War. Some of the proponents are irresponsible; most are merely misinformed. There are many substantial reasons why the UN has not dealt with the Vietnam conflict. Important among these is the one frequently asserted by U Thant: Communist China and the two Vietnams are not members. Most of the member states see no possibility that the UN can provide a useful framework for negotiation so long as China is absent. A majority of members are also opposed to Security Council consideration because they believe that it would lead to divisive and perhaps damaging debate, with no possibility for constructive action.

The United Nations could have a role if and when a negotiated settlement or a cease-fire is achieved. Then it might have a major responsibility in the conduct of relief and rehabilitation—particularly if furnished to both North and South Vietnam. The UN already has in operation a Mekong River project, and the UN Economic Commission for Asia and the Far East is concerned with Vietnam. A new organization along the lines of the post-World War II United Nations Relief and Rehabilitation Administration (UNRRA) or UNKRA in Korea may ultimately be required. The UN gained valuable experience in the conduct of civil operations in the Congo where the activities of all of the specialized agencies such as the World Health Organization and the Food and Agriculture Organization were coordinated under the direction of the Secretary-General as a single program.

It is also possible that during the process of de-escalation or after a cease-fire the UN might provide a peacekeeping force or an observation corps to oversee its implementation. This could, in time, include responsibility for supervising the conduct of a plebiscite or election. UN involvement in the political and security aspects of a settlement will depend considerably on the extent of participation and the attitude, at the time, of Communist China.

This raises the question of whether the United Nations should have a role in checking future insurgency or counterinsurgency. The US use of these terms has referred to Communist controlled or inspired action, but the terms need not be so limited. If a government calls for UN help before an insurgency has developed into large-scale guerrilla warfare, it is possible to imagine a desirable and effective UN role. If the action required were limited to border observation or regular police and paramilitary functions such as riot control, a UN role might be envisaged. The mechanics of providing for a sufficiently rapid peacekeeping action by the United Nations are not insurmountable, even under present circumstances.

More difficult to achieve will be the necessary political consensus within the Security Council, which will not vote authority to quell a revolution or block an insurgency unless there is persuasive evidence of a real threat to the international peace. The critical factor, in most cases, will be the demonstration of outside support for the insurgency. Even then, a military dictator who calls for help to prevent the overthrow of his government will not get it if a majority of UN members believes the revolutionary action is genuinely popular. In some circumstances, though, it is possible to contemplate Security Council authorization of a peacekeeping force or observer mission if a government requests help, and if there are strong indications that the situation might escalate, and if the action could be taken without requiring combat.

Proposals: United States Measures

POLICY. In an address in April, 1966, entitled "A Fresh Look at the UN," Joseph J. Sisco, Assistant Secretary of State for

International Organization Affairs, said: "We consider UN peacekeeping an important security option in US foreign policy. The UN has undertaken some dozen peacekeeping operations—all of which have served the national interests of the United States and the cause of peace.... For our part, we will support desirable future peacekeeping operations. We recognize that where a major power has fundamental objections, those who favor a particular operation may have to carry a heavier financial burden." Mr. Sisco's use of the word "desirable" implies that the United States believes the UN may authorize some undesirable operations. Commentary in the US press has reflected concern about the number of so-called "mini-states" entering the UN and the growing number of irresponsible resolutions approved in the General Assembly by states that, though numerous, represent an infinitesimal fraction of the world's power. However, because the Third World has too much at stake in the UN to risk its emasculation, those nations will probably listen carefully to Mr. Sisco's warning and will not force authorization of operations the United States considers unacceptable.

This question of responsibility is not one-sided. Charles W. Yost, former US Ambassador and Deputy Representative to the United Nations, made this clear in his excellent article, "The United Nations: Crisis of Confidence and Will," in the October, 1966, issue of *Foreign Affairs:*

> ... the responsibility for making the Assembly "work" does not rest solely with the Afro-Asians. Western statesmen sometimes imagine that if Afro-Asians would only act "responsibly"—that is, in a manner inoffensive to Western interests and sensibilities—the world would proceed smoothly along its accustomed dichotomous course and the General Assembly would continue to reflect the comforting consensus which existed there before 1960. Yet such statesmen in their less euphoric moments recognize that "winds of change" are blowing, and the "town meeting of the world" cannot escape the blast. The Afro-Asians will in fact be "responsible" and the Assembly will "work" to the extent that the developed Western nations offer within its framework an acceptable measure of satisfaction to the vital interests of the

Afro-Asians, especially in the fields of trade and aid, human rights and decolonization. Their task in doing so will certainly not be facilitated either by the failure of Britain and the United Nations to check "white settler" domination of Rhodesia or by the recent politically inspired decision of the International Court of Justice on South West Africa, both of which have substantially contributed to the growing and dangerous African impression that they cannot find justice through the United Nations. . . .

The US position on peacekeeping as reflected in the speeches of Ambassador Goldberg and Mr. Sisco is still very affirmative, but more defensive in tone than in the past. This is understandable in view of the Article 19 debacle, the Vietnam War, the Dominican intervention, and the ensuing decline in US popularity at the United Nations. It is true, too, that senior US officials preoccupied with the day-to-day developments in the war have not had much time to consider the future of UN peacekeeping. It is also true that, so long as the war continues, there is little prospect for agreed action to improve peacekeeping machinery. Nevertheless a number of things might usefully be pursued within the US government.

One of the most important first steps would be a decision by the President to give higher priority to UN peacekeeping, and to consider it under appropriate circumstances as a substitute for US action. Implicit in such a decision would be the recognition that Soviet acquiescence will be required, though it is possible that the General Assembly might act over Soviet objection on a minor issue. Since the Soviets have sometimes acquiesced very reluctantly to peacekeeping forces, their support in the future can perhaps be relied upon with more assurance if they are allowed to assume a greater responsibility for the success of UN peacekeeping and if they are given reason to develop greater trust in the impartiality of the Secretary-General and the peacekeeping process.

One step that might contribute to a better understanding of the different approaches to peacekeeping would be for the

United States to agree to an examination of proposals set forth for the first time in the Soviet memorandum of July, 1964, and reiterated in the policy statement of March, 1967. The Soviet position is that a great number of states should be added to the Military Staff Committee of the Security Council to participate in the strategic direction and the operational command of a UN force. The Soviets have suggested that the Military Staff Committee could establish regional peacekeeping bodies for the various regions of the world. They urge measures to enhance the capacity of the Security Council to act swiftly and effectively. An exploration of this position by a subcommittee of the Security Council might provide the basis for a compromise. The United States might agree that the Soviet formula be applied to all UN operations involving enforcement by military combat, while the Soviet Union might agree that peacekeeping operations and observer missions designed to prevent the use of force could be managed, as they have been in the past, by the Secretary-General with broad authority usually provided by the Security Council.

Such an agreement would not really change anything, including the sources of authority provided in the Charter, but it might reassure the Soviet Union that the UN would not engage in combat operations directed against its interests. The United States also would probably have to accept the inclusion of Communist units in some future peacekeeping forces in some areas of the world. When this occurs there would have to be some involvement of Communists in the command of a force, and greater participation at UN headquarters by Soviet and Eastern European members of the Secretariat staff.

Another change that might promote Soviet backing would be to take the counsel of Professor Inis Claude of the University of Michigan, who suggests that US interests would be better served if UN operations are considered impartial, with both the United States and the Soviet Union using the organization to control and block disputes, rather than to advance Communism or anti-Communism. Other organizations and sources of power are much better suited to the waging or containing of the Cold War. Keeping the UN peacekeeping function out of major US-Soviet disputes is not so impractical as it may seem, particularly when viewed in the context of the strategic interests shared by both superpowers in the face of the growing threat from China. In fact, the problem of China gives special urgency to the need for an accommodation between the United States and the Soviet Union with respect to UN peacekeeping.

CONTINGENCY PLANNING. UN peacekeeping should become an explicit subject for US contingency planning. For example, though the United States prefers the OAS for future peacekeeping in Latin America, it will nevertheless be desirable to consider the employment of the UN for western hemisphere peacekeeping. One of the fundamental barriers to the creation of an OAS standing force is the fear of domination by the United States. But under the UN an effective peace force can be formed without US participation. An acceptable force could be composed, for instance, of units from Canada and several Latin countries. It is sometimes forgotten that when the Secretary-General organizes a peacekeeping force, he selects national contingents acceptable to the host government and to other governments most directly involved. Obviously the Secretary-General would consult with the United States before selecting units to be assigned to a mission in the Caribbean. The fear that the Soviets would have a presence in the western hemisphere if a UN force were sent there is not valid. The US would not agree to the inclusion of East European Communists in a force for the western hemisphere, just as the Soviets would object to units from NATO countries in East Germany, for example. In the unlikely event that a Latin American host country did agree to the participation of a Communist unit, it is most unlikely that the Secretary-General would include it in the force if the United States strongly objected.

At the present time the Policy Planning Council of the Department of State has one man assigned to spend a portion of his time on the implications of UN peacekeeping for US policy. The importance of this subject warrants at least one full-time planner. It also merits more attention from the staffs of the US Representative to the United Nations and the Assistant Secretary for International Organization Affairs. The Defense Department should include consideration of UN peacekeeping in the planning functions of both the Office of the Secretary and the Joint Chiefs of Staff. Senior policy-makers have not become accustomed to thinking of UN action as one of the options they should always consider.

UN peacekeeping should become a part of the US crisis management machinery, with interagency policy and operating coordination assigned to the Assistant Secretary for International Organization Affairs. The crisis management machinery in the Defense Department should include personnel who are fully briefed in all aspects of peacekeeping, with emphasis on the capabilities of the earmarking states and those others most likely to make major contributions. At the present time there are several military officers assigned to represent the United States in the dormant Military Staff Committee. They report directly to the Joint Chiefs of Staff. Consideration should be given to broadening their responsibility toward the contingency planning aspect of the military implications of UN peacekeeping, and to having them report not only to the US Representative to the United Nations and the Joint Chiefs, but also to the Secretary of Defense.

One of the most vital aspects of successful crisis management is early warning. Occasionally the Secretary-General himself goes on a fact-finding mission. At other times he assigns personal representatives to report from trouble spots that may be a threat to the peace. More such fact-finding can and should be done, but the principal sources of data will continue to be the member governments. Unless a government asks for help in time, the conflict may develop beyond the point when UN action can be realistically contemplated. An emergency session of the Security Council can be called within twenty-four hours, and a vote is possible a few hours thereafter if the major powers are in accord. Usually, though, on any important issue a minimum of two or three days may be required. After the Council acts, several more days will be required for the Secretary-General to form a force and for that force to arrive in the field. Thus it is probably not practical to think of UN action in less than a week and usually it will require more time than that. Given circumstances where there is a realistic possibility of timely UN action, the United States should be prepared to press for that alternative. For example, when the Congolese government in 1960 appealed to the US for help, President Eisenhower advised it to go to the UN. The President's decision proved to be a wise one. Had he decided to intervene directly with US forces the crisis might have been rapidly resolved, but it is possible too that thousands of American troops might still be bogged down today—in the heart of Africa.

ASSISTANCE PROGRAMS. The United States should consider affirmative action on the proposal made by leaders of the Republican party that the US formally commit itself to providing airlift for UN operations through the facilities of the Military Air Transport Service, and that it earmark a unit of noncombat officers and men with specialized skills, such as medical corpsmen, engineers, seabees, etc. This proposal has the advantage of stimulating bipartisan endorsement of US involvement in UN peacekeeping and demonstrates an additional commitment of the US to UN operations. It should be recognized that, at this stage, the Soviets will probably object to any direct US participation, even though limited to technicians. It would be essential to explore this matter with the Secretary-General before making any public commitment.

There has been inadequate effort by the US government to use the authority in the Foreign Assistance Act that permits granting military assistance to enable recipient countries to "participate in collective measures requested by the UN for the purpose of maintaining or restoring international peace and security." Interviews with representatives of UN permanent missions revealed that none of the missions, including those from governments presently receiving US military assistance, was aware of this authority, though it has been mentioned in at least one speech by a State Department representative. According to senior officials in the Department of Defense, there has not yet been a decision within the government to relate defense assistance programs to the need to strengthen the peacekeeping capability of the United Nations. This situation is consistent with the preoccupation in the government, at least since 1964, with the direct use of US power and bilateral arrangements.

As Lincoln Bloomfield says in his article on peacekeeping in the July, 1966, *Foreign Affairs:*

> ... it cannot be repeated too often that American military assistance to under-developed countries might be far better invested if it emphasized the aim, already written into the legislation, of improving the capacity of international organizations to carry out peacekeeping functions. Such a shift in emphasis would strengthen those internal-security and civil action functions that appear far more useful than the status-symbol types of weapons which with depressing frequency wind up being used against internal rivals or close neighbors.

Some skeptics about the advisability of using US aid for UN-related purposes have raised the question of whether we would be accused of training and equipping US mercenaries for UN service. This might be a genuine problem for some recipients. But it should be recalled that nations that contribute units to UN peacekeeping serve under the UN flag, not the US flag, and they serve under authority granted by a political consensus of the members of the Security Council or the General Assembly in accordance with the law of the United Nations Charter. When Ambassador Arthur Goldberg said in November, 1965, that aid to earmarking nations could be made available through the UN, he did not specify what he meant. One possibility would be to create a "special earmarkers' fund" for the Secretary-General that he could use at his discretion to assist poorer countries who desire to earmark units for UN service.

The US Foreign Aid Program provides financial assistance and know-how to thirty-three nations to help them develop their civilian police. These programs have concentrated on such things as the maintenance of public order, border control, customs procedures, gendarmerie and paramilitary units to deal with bandits and small insurgencies. Though the civilian police skills developed in this program are clearly relevant to the requirements for civilian police in UN peacekeeping, there has been no consideration given to encouraging recipient governments to volunteer trained civilian police for UN service. Civilian police from countries like Nigeria and Ghana have already carried out important assignments for the United Nations. Even token numbers of well-trained policemen from some of the developing countries can make useful contributions and add balance to the participation in peacekeeping forces.

Arms requirements are growing throughout the world with serious negative implications for international peace and economic development. Most of the new African nations used to receive security protection from their European metropoles. Now there is a security vacuum. Many of these countries have begun to build up their military establishments, engaging in a race for arms even though they desperately need all of their financial resources for economic development. If the United Nations became strong enough to provide reliable, impartial peacekeeping, some of the poor nations might give less attention to military security, while concentrating on their priority needs of economic, social, and political development. This will not happen until the UN has built more reliable machinery than exists today—which is another important reason for strengthening the peacekeeping potential.

CONGRESS AND THE FINANCING OF PEACEKEEPING. Despite the irritation and frustration resulting from the long, drawn-out Article 19 controversy, the overwhelming majority of Congressmen have supported the United Nations in general and peacekeeping in particular. Congress has always followed the lead of the Executive Branch, providing whatever authority and funds have been requested. Since the funds for contributions to the UN come from either the State Department or the Foreign Aid appropriations, there has sometimes been a danger that Congressional cuts in these budgets might reduce the contributions. But so far that has not occurred.

In fact, Congress is sometimes ahead of the Executive Branch, as it was when it provided authority for US defense assistance to nations requiring it in order to contribute to UN collective security measures. Each year members of Congress sponsor bills or resolutions urging more "teeth" for UN peacekeeping. Recent recommendations urged "a permanent UN organization for such purposes as observation and patrol in situations that threaten international peace and security"; or said, "The Congress reaffirms its support for a permanent UN peacekeeping force." It is probably premature to consider the establishment of even a small permanent force, but these Congressional resolutions do indicate growing interest in the subject among some of the members.

There are strong and active groups of Republicans and Democrats in the House of Representatives who have shown a growing concern for strengthening the potential of UN peacekeeping.

Some of them have originated imaginative and constructive proposals for Executive Branch consideration. In the Senate there is bipartisan support for UN peace operations, particularly in the Senate Foreign Relations Committee. Each year two Congressmen participate for three months as members of the US delegation to the General Assembly—one year the members are from the Senate Foreign Relations Committee, the next year from the House Foreign Affairs Committee. In this manner a number of members of Congress, through the years, have become well versed in the workings of the United Nations. With a few exceptions, they have come away favorably impressed with the experience.

Sometimes the assertion is heard, particularly since the Article 19 debate, that Congress will cut appropriations for UN peacekeeping. But the record shows the contrary to be true. Except for the major debate over the bond issue to finance the force in the Congo, there has been little opposition in Congress to financial support for peacekeeping. A few critics have charged that the United States pays more than its share. Actually, when members' payments are measured as percentages of their own gross national products, twenty-one countries contribute proportionately more than the United States does. US contributions to the regular budget, which were limited by Congressional action in 1952 to 33⅓ percent, could easily be increased without making them disproportionate, because the US share of the world's gross product is now around 44 percent. US contributions to the major peacekeeping operations have been closer to this figure: 40 percent for Cyprus, 42 percent for the Congo, and 43 percent for UNEF. Since almost all US financing of peacekeeping is now handled through voluntary contributions, there is no reason why the United States cannot provide a larger part of the total cost of future operations, if that should prove desirable.

When an operation is clearly in the interest of US national security, the United States does not have much difficulty raising the money. For example, it was willing to pay almost the entire cost of the OAS peacekeeping mission in the Dominican Republic. It could, if necessary, do the same thing for the costs of the UN Cyprus operation. The Congress has year after year granted the full amount of the money requested by the Administration for defense spending. If the Secretary of Defense and/or the Joint Chiefs of Staff informed Congress, as they certainly would, that a particular UN peacekeeping operation was clearly in the US interest, there is not much question that Congress would appropriate the necessary funds. There is no real issue in Congress on this subject.

The main reason for keeping the US contribution to peacekeeping somewhere in the neighborhood of 45 to 50 percent is the desirability of broader financial participation by other states. Having a share in the financing of an operation does increase the commitment, even if for some of the poorer governments the amount is token. If the UN became too reliant on US contributions there might be negative political repercussions. The more governments there are making voluntary contributions to finance an operation, the less vulnerable the organization is to charges that UN peacekeepers are US mercenaries. Such charges are and always have been false, but some governments nevertheless may avoid volunteering for peacekeeping because of possible domestic political repercussions resulting from such accusations. This may be more of a problem for some of the neutral governments. It will become less of a factor if, and when, some of the Eastern European states become more involved in some of the operations.

For the foreseeable future UN peacekeeping will probably be financed by voluntary contributions rather than assessments. The United States should encourage maximum participation by the members in sharing the costs. One financing technique that would probably further this goal and that has not yet been tried for peacekeeping is an annual pledging conference of the entire membership of the General Assembly. Pledges could be made to cover the costs of each on-going peacekeeping operation. Presumably some states might support some operations and not others. If this technique were used it would mean that any nation could opt out if it had political objections to an operation. Since 1950 the pledging conference method has worked well in financing the UN technical assistance and pre-investment programs—now merged as the United Nations Development Program. In the early years the Soviet Union and the other Communist states, except Yugoslavia, did not contribute. But they have all supported the program recently, making their financial contributions in local currency. In 1966 all but seven of the 122 UN members pledged contributions to the budget of the Development Program for a total amount of $170 million. US pledges are limited by Congress to a maximum of 40 percent of the total given. Since peacekeeping operations are more controversial than development programs, pledging support for them probably will not be so widespread. Forty-four nations have financed the costs of the Cyprus operation. That number might be significantly increased if the pledging technique were used. But whatever the technique, the important thing to remember is that if there is broad political backing for a particular UN operation the money will be found. Money follows political consent, not vice versa.

Proposals: United Nations Measures

The vote of confidence given Secretary-General U Thant when all but one of the UN members supported him to remain on the job for a second term provided dramatic evidence that it is possible for a man to manage such politically sensitive matters as peacekeeping operations and still maintain the respect and confidence of most of the members. In 1966–67 the Secretary-General had two major frustrations, which he emphasized in the introduction to his annual report to the General Assembly and in the press conference he held when the report was released. His greatest torment has been the Vietnam War. He said:

> ...I believe it to be the first duty of the membership to face up to the fact that the chances of fruitful international co-operation on many crucial issues in which the United Nations has a clear responsibility for decision and action—issues ranging from disarmament to development—have been steadily and seriously impaired over the past two years by a situation over which, for well-known reasons, the United Nations has not been able to exercise any effective control. This situation, of course, is the deepening crisis over Viet-Nam, where the dangerous escalation of armed force has been accompanied, in my view, by an increasing intransigence and distrust among governments and peoples.

The other important preoccupation of the Secretary-General is the question of his authority. At his press conference he said he found it difficult to function effectively because some governments were treating him like a "glorified clerk." He was referring to the fact that the Soviets and the French have constantly challenged his executive role in the security field. U Thant believes that it is essential for the Secretary-General to be granted enough latitude to take "political and diplomatic initiatives."

On both of these issues—the Vietnam War and Soviet and French intransigence with respect to accepting essential executive responsibilities for the Secretary-General—there is a bind. The bind gets tighter as the war escalates. Until the situation eases there is no reason to hope that the Soviets and French will modify their position. U Thant, recognizing this political reality, has not pressed for institutional improvements in the Secretariat peacekeeping machinery. There is no substantial evidence that the Soviets and French will become more flexible about UN peacekeeping even after a cease-fire in Vietnam, but if the end of the fighting should lead to a genuine détente the prospects would be much brighter than they are today.

Some day, if and when the impasse is broken, there are several improvements that should be made. Presently, the Secretary-General is supported by an absurdly small Military Adviser's Office of one man. The Military Adviser's Office should be given a broader mandate and should be expanded by several officers so that it can prepare manuals on such subjects as earmarking, command and control, logistical support, etc. These manuals should provide the basis for establishing standard operating procedures for the military aspects of all future peacekeeping.

There is also a need for expanding the staff of senior Secretariat personnel responsible for the political direction and management of peacekeeping operations. Ralph Bunche and José Rolz-Bennett, who are most directly responsible for the administration of peacekeeping operations, have accomplished miracles with a very small staff. Because their work is so sensitive politically it is understandable that they have not wanted to disturb it with questions of personnel replacement and expansion. But these able and experienced men need more assistance, even in the conduct of present operations. If the UN is going to have the capacity for efficient and effective response to future calls for peacekeeping, several new men are required—most of them of relatively high rank because of the responsibilities involved. There is also a need for expansion of the Field Service and for trained men from the Secretariat who can serve in the field directing the civil aspects of peacekeeping operations.

In time the United Nations Institute for Training and Research should assume responsibilities in the peacekeeping field. UNITAR, which has the advantage of being independently financed and directed, should be able to engage in those aspects of strengthening the institution of peacekeeping that temporarily may be too controversial for the Secretariat. For example, a useful function it could fulfill would be to arrange for thorough analysis of all of the major peacekeeping operations of the past in order to learn lessons for the future and to develop material for training programs. UNITAR might be the best institution to start small training programs for military officers of member governments that would like to prepare for future peacekeeping assignments. Such a program, even if the course were only for one or two months, could prepare officers for the special responsibilities of command in a peacekeeping force, preparation not usually available in most officer training programs. UNITAR could, in time, establish an operations research arm that could assess alternative peacekeeping approaches and their applicability to the various areas likely to require peacekeeping in the future.

It may prove desirable to establish a UN Military Staff College under the auspices of UNITAR or independently. A staff college would be especially valuable if several additional nations decide to earmark forces for UN use, particularly if they are developing countries. Command of multinational forces can be improved, both at headquarters and in the field, if a single staff system is used. Another advantage of a staff college would be the bringing together of officers who would be working together in the future. It would facilitate the development of an inventory of skills and experience, which would be invaluable in the formation of peacekeeping forces.

All of the foregoing are measures that should considerably strengthen the machinery for peacekeeping. The US government can act at once to perfect its own machinery, but some of the other institutional improvements will have to await changes in the Soviet and possibly the French positions. In the meantime, the United Nations will go on responding to crisis with a military force improvised to meet the requirements of the particular dispute with the available resources. Because the UN has had considerable experience in peacekeeping, such improvisation will probably be relatively effective. UN peacekeeping will never provide the sort of reliable, efficient, controlled substitute for US military forces that some planners demand, but for political and pragmatic reasons it will on occasion be the least unattractive alternative. And as the machinery for peacekeeping improves, it should become a progressively more attractive alternative.

Ambassador Arthur Goldberg, speaking before the Special Political Committee on November 24, 1965, said:

> . . . the crucial ingredient in the United Nations' capacity to keep the peace does not lie in particular arrangements. The crucial ingredient is political and moral. It is our determination to rely on the United Nations, to use the United Nations, to have confidence in the United Nations' operating capacity. The stakes are so high that we should be willing to take chances on the United Nations' capacity to act, and to back it up even when some of its particular decisions go against our immediate national desires. For the risks of a United Nations without the capacity to act are far greater than the risk of a United Nations with that capacity.
>
> Let us put our faith in this Organization's ability to take on increasingly difficult peacekeeping tasks around the globe. It will make mistakes. It will annoy all of us some time, and some of us all the time. Despite these frustrations, we should be willing to risk reliance on United Nations peacekeeping, because the alternative—of immobilizing the United Nations in one of its key areas of activity—is too great a risk for us to take. It conjures up the specter of uncontained disorder and violence which could escalate into a world holocaust. . . .

Appendixes

APPENDIX A

Synopsis of Major Peacekeeping Operations

Greece

The United Nations' first peacekeeping venture occurred in response to Greek complaints to the Security Council in December, 1946, that its northern borders were being violated by neighboring Albania, Bulgaria, and Yugoslavia, each of which was allegedly assisting guerrillas in Greece. Within thirty days a commission, authorized by the Security Council, began on-the-scene investigations. UN action on the commission's recommendations was prevented, however, by a series of Soviet vetoes in the Security Council.

At US insistence the issue was brought before the veto-free General Assembly, which established in October, 1947, a United Nations Special Committee on the Balkans (UNSCOB). UNSCOB was empowered not only to investigate and report on the border situation but also to provide the parties with mediation assistance.

In 1952 Greece's northern borders became relatively quiet, and UNSCOB was replaced by a subcommission of the Peace Observation Commission that the General Assembly had established earlier under the Uniting for Peace resolution. The UN presence in Greece was terminated in August, 1954.

Palestine

During the twelve months preceding the expiration of the British Mandate for Palestine in May, 1948, various UN bodies, commissions, and authorized individuals sought to facilitate a Jewish-Arab settlement concerning the future of Palestine. All attempts failed, and within hours after the Provisional Government of Israel declared independence on May 15, neighboring Arab states invaded Palestine.

After a brief cease-fire collapsed in July, the Security Council ordered another, this time under Chapter VII of the Charter. Negotiations under UN auspices commenced early in 1949 between Israel and each of its four Arab neighbors—Egypt, Jordan, Lebanon, and

Syria. By July of the same year, each of these states had concluded an armistice agreement with Israel. Included in the implementation machinery for each agreement and for Security Council resolutions was a United Nations Truce Supervision Organization (UNTSO), with authority to report on observance of cease-fires and armistice agreements.

UNTSO supplies UN observers on all of Israel's borders except those with Egypt. After the war in 1956, UNTSO's functions on this border were taken over by the United Nations Emergency Force (UNEF) that was located in Gaza and Sinai.

Indonesia

Disagreements between the Netherlands and the Republic of Indonesia over the implementation of the Indonesian independence agreement formally signed by the two parties in March, 1947, led to military hostilities in the early summer of that year. In August, at the request of Indonesia, the Security Council called for a cease-fire and established a Good Offices Committee to assist in carrying it out. The Committee was aided by a small group of military observers from the staffs of the Consuls General in Indonesia. After the cease-fire broke down several times, a truce agreement was negotiated with UN assistance in January, 1948. This too failed to hold, and hostilities resumed during the final weeks of 1948.

In January, 1949, the Security Council again requested a cessation of the fighting, and reconstituted the earlier Commission as the United Nations Commission for Indonesia (UNCI), also with a complement of military observers. Agreements were reached in November, 1949, embodying a Dutch transfer of sovereignty to Indonesia. After completing its tasks regarding implementation of the transfer agreement, the UN mission was disbanded in early 1951.

Kashmir

When India and Pakistan became independent shortly after World War II, they divided between them some five hundred "states" formerly under British sovereignty. One of these, Kashmir, has been a source of bitter antagonism ever since its Hindu leader opted in 1947 for attaching his predominantly Moslem state to India.

In January, 1948, India accused Pakistan in the Security Council of sponsoring raids in Kashmir. The Council acted by establishing a United Nations Commission for India and Pakistan (UNCIP), whose authorization included investigating and reporting as well as assisting mediation efforts.

By January, 1949, the parties reached agreements that permitted a cease-fire. To assist UNCIP in overseeing the cease-fire, a group of military observers became operational almost immediately. They have come to be known as the United Nations Military Observer Group in India and Pakistan (UNMOGIP), which today has responsibilities for maintaining the uneasy truce in Kashmir.

Egypt

In late October, 1956, Israel, France, and Great Britain launched concerted attacks against Egypt. Security Council action to restore peace and secure troop withdrawals was prevented by French and British vetoes. Consequently, with US and Soviet acquiescence, Yugoslavia invoked the provisions of the Uniting for Peace resolution and transferred the issue to the General Assembly.

During the first week of November, the Assembly adopted a cease-fire resolution and authorized Secretary-General Hammarskjold to plan a peace force. The parties agreed, a cease-fire went into effect, and the Assembly created the United Nations Emergency Force (UNEF). Ten countries voluntarily provided troops, which numbered as many as 6,000 at one point—the first example of UN peace-keeping by comparatively large-scale military forces. These nonfighting units patrolled within Egypt along the Israeli borders in the Gaza Strip and the Sinai desert until May, 1967, when Egypt requested their withdrawal.

Lebanon

In May, 1958, Lebanon went before the Security Council to charge the United Arab Republic with massive intervention in its internal affairs, with infiltrating men and arms, and with conspiring through financial and other means against the Lebanese government. The Security Council waited to see whether the League of Arab States would be able to ease tensions. It could not, so the Council acted in early July to dispatch the United Nations Observer Group in Lebanon (UNOGIL) to ensure that no infiltration was occurring.

Middle East tensions increased in mid-July with the overthrow of the King in Iraq. Lebanon and Jordan immediately called for—and received—military support from the United States and Great Britain respectively.

Great-power differences stymied the Security Council, and an emergency session of the Assembly was convened. The United States and Great Britain agreed to withdraw their troops. By November the withdrawals were completed, elections had stabilized Lebanon's internal situation, and the borders were quiet. UNOGIL terminated operations by mid-December.

Congo

The largest, costliest, and most complex UN peacekeeping operation was a product of the chaos that followed the Congo's attainment of independence at the beginning of July, 1960. Within two weeks the army mutinied, law and order broke down completely, Katanga seceded, and the central government requested help from the United Nations. Secretary-General Hammarskjold requested the Security Council to act urgently. It responded by authorizing the United Nations Congo Operation (ONUC), with the United States and the Soviet Union voting affirmatively.

Utilizing civilian as well as military components, ONUC was authorized during the next four years to maintain law, order, and essential services throughout the Congo. Eventually, ONUC was granted authority by the Security Council to use force if necessary to perform its functions.

At its peak ONUC consisted of almost 20,000 military and specialized personnel contributed by 35 countries. ONUC cost the United Nations approximately $402 million. It was partly for financial reasons that ONUC was forced to withdraw completely in the summer of 1964.

West Irian

The main problem left unresolved by the Indonesian accession to independence in 1949 was the status of the territory of West New Guinea (West Irian). The Dutch continued to administer the area despite Indonesian claims that the territory was an integral part of

Indonesia. After more than a decade of political wrangling, Indonesians and Dutch clashed in minor military episodes during late 1961 and early 1962.

Negotiations in and outside the UN brought an agreement in August, 1962, governing the terms of an immediate relinquishment of Dutch sovereignty, an interim period of control by the UN, and an eventual transfer of administrative authority to Indonesia, to be held until a plebiscite in 1969.

Even before the UN formally acted to implement the agreement, the Secretary-General's military adviser and a small observer unit arrived in West New Guinea to assist in the immediate tasks of implementation. One month later, in September, 1962, the General Assembly authorized the establishment of the United Nations Temporary Executive Authority (UNTEA). UNTEA maintained local security and, under the ultimate authority of the Secretary-General, fully administered West New Guinea until Indonesia took over in May, 1963. In addition to a core of UN officials, UNTEA comprised a security force of some 1,500 Pakistani troops, as well as local military personnel who were temporarily placed under UNTEA's command.

Yemen

Throughout 1962 Yemen was caught up in a civil war between royalist and republican factions, supported directly and actively by Saudi Arabia and the UAR, respectively. Diplomatic missions from the United Nations and the United States managed by early 1963 to arrange a disengagement agreement under which the warring parties and their supporters would cease military activity and undertake a phased withdrawal of forces.

To supervise the disengagement and to police demilitarized zones, the Security Council created the United Nations Yemen Observation Mission (UNYOM). The enabling resolution was adopted in June, 1963, and observers arrived in Yemen within several weeks with authority to certify whether the parties were complying with the agreement. Despite extremely difficult physical conditions, they were able to report that compliance, particularly on the part of the UAR, was minimal. Without authority to force a solution on the parties, UNYOM's functions therefore could not be performed. Accordingly it was withdrawn in September, 1964.

Cyprus

Greek and Turkish Cypriot communities entered a period of fragile and irregular cooperation following Cypriot independence in 1960. Internecine rivalry between the preponderant Greeks and the minority Turks erupted into violent fighting during Christmas week of 1963.

Immediate tasks of maintaining peace fell to the British, whose troops were already in Cyprus by treaty right. After attempts to reach agreement on a NATO peacekeeping force failed during the early months of 1964, largely because of resistance by Cypriot President Archbishop Makarios, the UN acted in March. Without objection by any of the great powers, the Security Council authorized the formation of a United Nations Force in Cyprus (UNFICYP), which became operational in late March. Since then, the Security Council has regularly extended UNFICYP's mandate to remain on the island.

Nine countries have provided military units or small contingents of civilian police, which at their peak numbered nearly 7,000. These forces are responsible for assisting in the maintenance of law and order and for normalizing conditions on the island.

India-Pakistan

War broke out between India and Pakistan in August, 1965, and the matter was soon brought before the Security Council for action. After the parties ignored its calls for a cease-fire during the first week of September, the Council used exceptionally strong language and, with the consent of the United States and the Soviet Union, demanded a cease-fire and a subsequent withdrawal of military forces. Three days later a cease-fire formally went into effect.

The Council delegated to the Secretary-General the responsibility for assisting in the supervision of the cease-fire agreement. He strengthened the existing UN observers in Kashmir (UNMOGIP), and created a new group to patrol the borders between India and Pakistan, for which UNMOGIP had no responsibility. The new machinery was called the United Nations India-Pakistan Observation Mission (UNIPOM).

UNIPOM commenced operations in late September, 1965, and remained on the scene until its functions had been completed in March, 1966. UNIPOM was then disbanded; UNMOGIP has continued its role in Kashmir.

APPENDIX B

Selected Articles from the United Nations Charter

Chapter I: Purposes and Principles

ARTICLE 1

1. To maintain international peace and security, and to that end: to take effective collective measures for the prevention and removal of threats to the peace, and for the suppression of acts of aggression or other breaches of the peace, and to bring about by peaceful means, and in conformity with the principles of justice and international law, adjustment or settlement of international disputes or situations which might lead to a breach of the peace. . . .

ARTICLE 2

7. Nothing contained in the present Charter shall authorize the United Nations to intervene in matters which are essentially within the domestic jurisdiction of any state or shall require the Members to submit such matters to settlement under the present Charter; but this principle shall not prejudice the application of enforcement measures under Chapter VII.

Chapter IV: The General Assembly

ARTICLE 11

2. The General Assembly may discuss any questions relating to the maintenance of international peace and security brought before it by any Member of the United Nations, or by the Security Council, or by a state which is not a Member of the United Nations in accordance with Article 35, paragraph 2, and, except as provided in Article 12, may make recommendations with regard to any such questions to the state or states concerned or to the Security Council or to both. Any such question on which action is necessary shall be referred to the Security Council by the General Assembly either before or after discussion.

ARTICLE 17

1. The General Assembly shall consider and approve the budget of the Organization.

2. The expenses of the Organization shall be borne by the Members as apportioned by the General Assembly.

ARTICLE 19

A Member of the United Nations which is in arrears in the payment of its financial contributions to the Organization shall have no vote in the General Assembly if the amount of its arrears equals or exceeds the amount of the contributions due from it for the preceding two full years. The General Assembly may, nevertheless, permit such a Member to vote if it is satisfied that the failure to pay is due to conditions beyond the control of the Member.

Chapter V: The Security Council

ARTICLE 24

1. In order to ensure prompt and effective action by the United Nations, its Members confer on the Security Council primary responsibility for the maintenance of international peace and security, and agree that in carrying out its duties under this responsibility the Security Council acts on their behalf.

ARTICLE 25

The Members of the United Nations agree to accept and carry out the decisions of the Security Council in accordance with the present Charter.

Chapter VI: Pacific Settlement of Disputes

ARTICLE 33

1. The parties to any dispute, the continuance of which is likely to endanger the maintenance of international peace and security, shall, first of all, seek a solution by negotiation, enquiry, mediation, conciliation, arbitration, judicial settlement, resort to regional agencies or arrangements, or other peaceful means of their own choice.

ARTICLE 36

1. The Security Council may, at any stage of a dispute of the nature referred to in Article 33 or of a situation of like nature, recommend appropriate procedures or methods of adjustment.

2. The Security Council should take into consideration any procedures for the settlement of the dispute which have already been adopted by the parties.

3. In making recommendations under this Article the Security Council should also take into consideration that legal disputes should as a general rule be referred by the parties to the International Court of Justice in accordance with the provisions of the Statute of the Court.

ARTICLE 37

1. Should the parties to a dispute of the nature referred to in Article 33 fail to settle it by the means indicated in that Article, they shall refer it to the Security Council.

2. If the Security Council deems that the continuance of the dispute is in fact likely to endanger the maintenance of international peace and security, it shall decide whether to take action under Article 36 or to recommend such terms of settlement as it may consider appropriate.

Chapter VII: Action With Respect to Threats to the Peace, Breaches of the Peace, and Acts of Aggression

ARTICLE 39

The Security Council shall determine the existence of any threat to the peace, breach of the peace, or act of aggression and shall make recommendations, or decide what measures shall be taken in accordance with Articles 41 and 42, to maintain or restore international peace and security.

ARTICLE 41

The Security Council may decide what measures not involving the use of armed force are to be employed to give effect to its decisions, and it may call upon the Members of the United Nations to apply such measures. These may include complete or partial interruption of economic relations and of rail, sea, air, postal, telegraphic, radio, and other means of communication, and the severance of diplomatic relations.

ARTICLE 42

Should the Security Council consider that measures provided for in Article 41 would be inadequate or have proved to be inadequate, it may take such action by air, sea, or land forces as may be necessary to maintain or restore international peace and security. Such action may include demonstrations, blockade, and other operations by air, sea, or land forces of Members of the United Nations.

ARTICLE 43

1. All Members of the United Nations, in order to contribute to the maintenance of international peace and security, undertake to make available to the Security Council, on its call and in accordance with a special agreement or agreements, armed forces, assistance, and facilities, including rights of passage, necessary for the purpose of maintaining international peace and security.

2. Such agreement or agreements shall govern the numbers and types of forces, their degree of readiness and general location, and the nature of the facilities and assistance to be provided.

3. The agreement or agreements shall be negotiated as soon as possible on the initiative of the Security Council. They shall be concluded between the Security Council and Members or between the Security Council and groups of Members and shall be subject to ratification by the signatory states in accordance with their respective constitutional processes.

ARTICLE 44

When the Security Council has decided to use force it shall, before calling upon a Member not represented on it to provide armed forces in fulfillment of the obligations assumed under Article 43, invite that Member, if the Member so desires, to participate in the decisions of the Security Council concerning the employment of contingents of that Member's armed forces.

ARTICLE 45

In order to enable the United Nations to take urgent military measures, Members shall hold immediately available national air-force contingents for combined international enforcement action. The strength and degree of readiness of these contingents and plans for their combined action shall be determined, within the limits laid down in the special agreement or agreements referred to in Article 43, by the Security Council with the assistance of the Military Staff Committee.

ARTICLE 47

1. There shall be established a Military Staff Committee to advise and assist the Security Council on all questions relating to the Security Council's military requirements for the maintenance of international peace and security, the employment and command of forces placed at its disposal, the regulation of armaments, and possible disarmament.

2. The Military Staff Committee shall consist of the Chiefs of Staff of the permanent members of the Security Council or their representatives. Any Member of the United Nations not permanently represented on the Committee shall be invited by the Committee to be associated with it when the efficient discharge of the Committee's responsibilities requires the participation of that Member in its work.

3. The Military Staff Committee shall be responsible under the Security Council for the strategic direction of any armed forces placed at the disposal of the Security Council. Questions relating to the command of such forces shall be worked out subsequently.

4. The Military Staff Committee, with the authorization of the Security Council and after consultation with appropriate regional agencies, may establish regional subcommittees.

Chapter VIII: Regional Arrangements

ARTICLE 52

1. Nothing in the present Charter precludes the existence of regional arrangements or agencies for dealing with such matters relating to the maintenance of international peace and security as are appropriate for regional action, provided that such arrangements or agencies and their activities are consistent with the Purposes and Principles of the United Nations.

2. The Members of the United Nations entering into such arrangements or constituting such agencies shall make every effort to achieve pacific settlement of local disputes through such regional arrangements or by such regional agencies before referring them to the Security Council.

3. The Security Council shall encourage the development of pacific settlement of local disputes through such regional arrangements or by such regional agencies either on the initiative of the states concerned or by reference from the Security Council.

4. This Article in no way impairs the application of Articles 34 and 35.

ARTICLE 54

The Security Council shall at all times be kept fully informed of activities undertaken or in contemplation under regional arrangements or by regional agencies for the maintenance of international peace and security.

Chapter XV: The Secretariat

ARTICLE 99

The Secretary-General may bring to the attention of the Security Council any matter which in his opinion may threaten the maintenance of international peace and security.

ARTICLE 100

1. In the performance of their duties the Secretary-General and the staff shall not seek or receive instructions from any government or from any other authority external to the Organization. They shall refrain from any action which might reflect on their position as international officials responsible only to the Organization.

2. Each Member of the United Nations undertakes to respect the exclusively international character of the responsibilities of the Secretary-General and the staff and not to seek to influence them in the discharge of their responsibilities.

Selected Bibliography

Books and Pamphlets

Bingham, June, *U Thant.* New York: Alfred A. Knopf, 1966.

Bloomfield, Lincoln P., ed. *International Military Forces.* Boston: Little, Brown & Co., 1964.

———. *The United Nations and U.S. Foreign Policy.* Boston: Little, Brown & Co., 1960.

Boyd, Andrew, *United Nations: Piety, Myth and Truth.* Harmondsworth, Middx., England: Penguin Special 5214, 1962.

Buchan, Alastair, *Crisis Management: The New Diplomacy.* (The Atlantic Papers, NATO Series II.) France: The Atlantic Institute, 1966.

Burns, Arthur Lee and Nina Heathcote, *Peace-keeping by UN Forces: From Suez to the Congo.* New York: Frederick A. Praeger, 1963.

Calvocoressi, Peter, *World Order and New States: Problems of Keeping the Peace.* London: Chatto & Windus (Institute for Strategic Studies), 1962.

Cox, Arthur M., and Karl Mathiasen III, *United Nations Institute for Training and Research.* Washington: Brookings Institution, 1964.

Dallin, Alexander, *The Soviet Union at the United Nations.* New York: Frederick A. Praeger, 1962.

Frydenberg, Per, ed. *Peace-keeping Experience and Evaluation.* Oslo: Norwegian Institute of International Affairs, 1964.

Frye, William R., *A United Nations Peace Force.* New York: Oceana Publications, 1957.

Gardner, Richard N., *In Pursuit of World Order.* New York: Frederick A. Praeger, 1964.

Landis, Captain Gary E., USN, *Blue Bonnets for Dr. Bunche: Some Aspects of Earmarked Military Forces for United Nations Duty.* Unpublished study, Seventh Senior Seminar for Foreign Policy, Foreign Service Institute. Washington: U.S. Department of State, 1965.

Lefever, Ernest W., *Crisis in the Congo: A United Nations Force in Action.* Washington: Brookings Institution, 1965.

McKay, Vernon, ed. *African Diplomacy.* New York: Frederick A. Praeger, 1966.

McVitty, Marion H., *The Constitutional Crisis of the United Nations.* New York: The Committee for World Development and World Disarmament, 1965.

Nyerere, Julius, *A United States of Africa.* New York: Barnes and Noble, 1964.

O'Brien, Conor Cruise, *To Katanga and Back: A UN Case History.* New York: Simon and Schuster, 1962.

Rikhye, I. J., *Preparation and Training of United Nations Peace-keeping Forces* (Adelphi Papers, No. 9). London: Institute for Strategic Studies, 1964.

Rosner, Gabriella, *The United Nations Emergency Force.* New York: Columbia University Press, 1963.

Russell, Ruth B., *United Nations Experience with Military Forces: Political and Legal Aspects.* Washington: Brookings Institution, 1964.

Stoessinger, John G., *Financing the United Nations System.* Washington: Brookings Institution, 1964.

———. *The United Nations and the Super-Powers.* New York: Random House, 1965.

Wainhouse, David W., and others, *International Peace Observation.* Baltimore: Johns Hopkins Press, 1966.

Wilcox, Francis O., and H. Field Haviland, Jr., *The United States and the United Nations.* Baltimore: Johns Hopkins Press, 1961.

Wood, David, *The Armed Forces of African States* (Adelphi Papers, No. 27). London: Institute for Strategic Studies, 1966.

Young, Oran R., *Trends in International Peacekeeping* (Research Monograph, No. 22). Princeton: Center of International Studies, Princeton University, 1966.

Articles

Bloomfield, Lincoln P., "Peacekeeping and Peacemaking," *Foreign Affairs,* Vol. 44, No. 4, July, 1966, pp. 671–682.

Cox, Arthur M., "What does 'UN Peacekeeping' Mean?" *The Saturday Review,* May 14, 1966, pp. 19–22.

Haekkerup, Per, "Scandinavia's Peace-Keeping Forces for the UN," *Foreign Affairs,* Vol. 42, No. 2, July, 1964, pp. 675–681.

Keohane, Robert O., "Political Influence in the General Assembly," *International Conciliation,* No. 557, March, 1966.

Yost, Charles W., "The United Nations: Crisis of Confidence and Will," *Foreign Affairs,* Vol. 45, No. 1, October, 1966, pp. 19–35.

Documents

United Nations General Assembly, Official Records: Twenty-first Session, *Analysis of the Finances of the United Nations.* Report by the Secretary-General (A/AC.124/1, 24 January 1966).

United Nations General Assembly, Official Records: Twenty-first Session, Suppl. No. 1A, *Introduction to the Annual Report of the Secretary-General on the Work of the Organization, 16 June 1965–15 June 1966.*

United Nations General Assembly, Official Records: Twenty-first Session, *Report of the Ad Hoc Committee of Experts to Examine the Finances of the United Nations and the Specialized Agencies* (A/6289, 28 March 1966, and Add. 1, 31 March 1966).

United Nations General Assembly, Official Records: Nineteenth Session, Annex No. 21, *Report of the Secretary-General and the President of the General Assembly*, p. 79.

United Nations Peacekeeping in the Congo: 1960–1964. 4 Vols. Prepared for the US Arms Control and Disarmament Agency by Ernest W. Lefever and Wynfred Joshua of the Foreign Policy Studies Division of the Brookings Institution, Washington, June 30, 1966.

U.S. Congress, House of Representatives, Subcommittee on International Organizations and Movements, Committee on Foreign Affairs. *United Nations Financial Situation: Background and Consequences of the Article 19 Controversy over the Financing of UN Peacekeeping Operations.* Report 89 Cong. 2 sess. Washington: Government Printing Office, 1966.

U.S.S.R. Memorandum on UN Peacekeeping, in Annex 21 to United Nations General Assembly, Official Records: Nineteenth Session (A/5721, 13 July 1964).

U.S.S.R. Memorandum on UN Peacekeeping, in United Nations Doc. A/6641, 11 April 1967.

Addresses

Jackson, Senator Henry M., "The U.S. in the United Nations: An Independent Audit." Washington: Address before the National Press Club, March 20, 1962.

McNamara, Robert S., Address before the American Society of Newspaper Editors, May 1966. *New York Times,* May 19, 1966, p. 11.

Sisco, Joseph J., "A Fresh Look at the UN" (Address before the Regional Foreign Policy Conference, Atlanta, Georgia, April 2, 1966). State Department Press Release No. 75, April 2, 1966.

Index

Index